**$4.95**

D1155430

The Homosexual Revolution:

A Look At The
Preachers And Politicians
Behind It

David A. Noebel

# The Homosexual Revolution:

# A Look At The Preachers And Politicians Behind It

Summit Press
MANITOU SPRINGS, CO 80829

# CONTENTS

Copyright, 1984, by Summit Ministries

All rights reserved. No part of this book may be reproduced or transmitted in any form or by any means, electronic or mechanical, including photocopying, recording, or by any information storage and retrieval system, without permission in writing from Summit Ministries.

First Edition, 5,000 copies printed, August, 1977.
Second Edition, 25,000 copies printed, January, 1978.
First Printing, 15,000 printed, January, 1979.
Second Printing, 10,000 printed, February, 1981.
Third Edition, 10,000 printed, March 1984.

Summit Press
P. O. Box 207
Manitou Springs, CO 80829

Printed in the United States of America

About the Author

David A. Noebel is president of Summit Ministries, an interdenominational training center for teenagers and their families in Manitou Springs, Colorado. He is listed in *Who's Who in Religion* and is a professional member of the American Philosophical Association.

"So God created man in his own image, in the image of God he created him; male and female created he them."

—Moses, Genesis 1:27.

"But from the beginning of the Creation God made them male and female. For this cause shall a man leave his father and mother, and cleave to his wife; and they twain shall be one flesh: so then they are no more twain, but one flesh. What therefore God hath joined together, let not man put asunder."

—Jesus, Mark 10:6-9

Preface

*"Americans want a vocal church on spiritual, moral, and ethical matters."*

George Gallup

*"Opposition to homosexuality is widespread among all groups in the population and is based on ethical grounds."*

Rev. Enrique T. Rueda
Author, **The Homosexual Network**

Men and women of good will are being called upon to rethink the homosexual issue. They are being asked to change their attitude, ethics, and the laws of the land to legitimize homosexuality.

The American Psychiatric Association, under pressure from homosexuals, already has removed homosexuality from its list of mental disorders—a move which Dr. Charles W. Socarides labeled "the psychiatric hoax of the century."[1] By suggesting that homosexuality is merely an alternative life style psychiatrists not only effectively tore down the traditional social taboos surrounding homosexual behavior, but virtually opened the flood gates which quickly resulted in homosexual promiscuity and the resultant gay plague stalking America today.

The Democratic National Committee has decided to work closely with the National Association of Gay and Lesbian Democratic Clubs toward the common goal of "achieving full human rights and civil rights for every American" and ending any "discrimination based on sexual orientation."[2] The Committee has encouraged the homosexuals to establish officially a "Lesbian and Gay Caucus" within the Democratic National Committee. It would take its place alongside the Black Caucus, the Women's Caucus, the Hispanic Caucus and the Progressive-Liberal Caucus.

Also, the Church is being asked to rethink its attitude toward homosexuals. "The Church," says John W. Drakeford in his book *A Christian View of Homosexuality,* "must realize that homosexuals, too, have been unfairly treated in the past. Most of the laws and practices which discriminate against homosexuals are obviously unfair."[3]

To remedy this situation, Drakeford admonishes us by stating, "There are many places within the life of the Church where homosexuals could fulfill important functions." But, says Drakeford, "If homosexuals feel attracted to children and adolescents, it probably would not be wise to have them working with either of these groups."[4]

Letha Scanzoni and Virginia Mollenkott in their work *Is The Homosexual My Neighbor?* take a more radical position than Drakeford. The two authors argue that "God may direct us to transcend time-honored moral guidelines or law" and since sexual orientation is not a matter of choice it is best to work for moral homosexual relationships or as they put it "a conventional homosexual relationship." Instead of the traditional view of fornication, adultery, promiscuity and homosexuality labeled sin, an alternative view is proposed which labels fornication, adultery and promiscuity sin for both heterosexual and homosexual persons. This falls under their chapter, "Proposing a Homosexual Christian Ethic," and is based on the premise that one should no more "deplore homosexuality than left-handedness."[5] Unbelievable as it may seem, Scanzoni and Mollenkott actually argue that "modern research has shown that homosexual contact is not at all 'unnatural' if we are going to use practices in the animal world as our criteria."[6]

It is the position of this author, as opposed to the above, that a true "Christian" viewpoint will insist: (a) that homosexuals should not be in the ministry, (b) that homosexuals should not be teaching children or adolescents, (c) that homosexuals should not be in the military, (d) that homosexuals should not be placed in national security positions, etc.

It is also the view of this work that homosexuals are not a minority in the same sense that negroes in America constitute a minority. For one thing, blacks can't help being black while homosexuals can help being homosexual. Homosexuals are a minority in the sense that aberrant social behavior is an activity of a minority. It is therefore the view of this book that homosexual behavior is not worthy of any special religious, political or legal consideration since such consideration only legitimizes the homosexual life style, hence causing many to miss the error of their ways, and confirming them in their homosexuality. When *Newsweek* (August 8, 1983) admits that being a male homosexual today is synonymous with being "afraid of catching AIDS" no one should be confirming anyone in the homosexual life style.

Unfortunately, over the past few years a powerful homosexual revolution has occurred, and the homosexuals are no longer content to remain in the closet. They are seeking positions in the ministry, the teaching professions, the military, and government—even the CIA. Assisting them in their revolution have been primarily the media (which are strongly pro-homosexual),[7] religious organizations (especially liberal clergy and the National Council of Churches), and politicians who are permissive toward homosexuality (primarily, though not exclusively, in the Democratic Party).

Today, the liberated, out of the closet homosexual lifestyle involves homosexual bars, homosexual bathhouses (both unique homosexual institutions), homosexual churches, homosexual support groups, homosexual political clubs, AIDS, veneral disease, Kaposi's sarcoma, S&M, drag queens, and pedophilia (homosexuals are constantly seeking to lower the age of sexual consent).

The militant homosexual movement is presently referred to as the gay liberation movement. According to the new breed of homosexuals, being homosexual is not synonymous with being gay. A closet homosexual (one who denies or conceals his homosexuality) is not liberated and hence not truly part of the gay movement. The traditional homosexual is contrasted with the liberated homosexual who is proud of his homosexual lifestyle. Hence, a traditional homosexual is one who is sexually attracted to another of his own sex, but a liberated homosexual is a member of the gay subculture. He or she takes pride in the subculture. Hence, a gay is a liberated homosexual living in the mainstream of gay life and culture.

The overriding desire of the gay liberation movement is to convince the non-homosexual that gay is good! That homosexuality is an alternative lifestyle on a par with the heterosexual lifestyle and that non-homosexuals should accept the homosexual lifestyle as normal, natural and even moral.

This book is written to explain why the vast majority of Americans regret the thesis that homosexuality is normal, moral, or good and why they feel the liberated homosexual is not worthy of special social, religious, political and legal protection or consideration.

1. *Time,* April 1, 1974, p. 45.
2. See Appendix 10.
3. John W. Drakeford, *A Christian View of Homosexuality* (Nashville, Tenn.: Broadman Press, 1977), p. 134.
4. *Ibid.*
5. Letha Scanzoni and Virginia Mollenkott, *Is The Homosexual My Neighbor?* (New York: Harper and Row, Publisher, 1980), p. 77.

6. *Ibid.,* p. 65.

7. *Colorado Springs Gazette Telegraph,* April 17, 1982, p. 18B. Study by Robert Lichter and Stanley Rothman found 75% of media staff approving of the homosexual lifestyle.

Introduction

*"The media have played down a number of facts that would be seriously damaging to the homosexual movement, though they are obvious to even a casual observer."*

*—Joseph Sobran*
*Syndicated Columnist*

Homosexuality is one of America's most serious moral and social problems. Homosexuals are marching in the nation's biggest protest demonstrations since the days of the antiwar movement. There are powerful forces, e.g., the National Gay Task Force and numerous local Gay Alliance groups, seeking to remove the stigma of being homosexual and equating homosexual life-styles with heterosexual life-styles.

The organized homosexual community is something worth considering and taking seriously. In just one publication we noted the following homosexual organizations: American Baptist Gay Caucus, Dignity, Friends Committee for Gay Concerns, Integrity, Lutherans Concerned, Unitarian-Universalist Gay Caucus, Evangelicals Concerned, Presbyterian Gay Caucus, Salvatorian, United Church of Christ Gay Caucus, Metropolitan Community Church, Moravians Concerned, United Methodist Gay Caucus, Gay Teachers Caucus, Gay Historians and Political Scientists, American Library Association Gay Task Force, Gay Academic Union, Gay Teachers Association, Gay Anthropologists, Gay Social Workers, Gay Caucus of the American Psychiatric Association, Association of Gay Psychologists, Gay Social Service Alliance, Gay Medical Students, Gay Nurses Association, Caucus of Gay Public Health Workers, The

Dorian Group, National Gay Prisoners Coalition, Chicago Gay Seminarians and Clergy, Gay Airline Pilots Association, Gay Public Employees Federation, Gay Rights Law Panel, Lambda Legal Defense Fund, Gay People's Legal Committee, Gay Law Collective, Gay Legal Caucuses, National Lawyers Guild Gay Caucus and Gay Law Students Association.

Enrique T. Rueda's work *The Homosexual Network* contains 49 pages of homosexual organizations—including political clubs, religious groups and orders, student groups, homosexual synagogues, support and interest groups. The listings run into the hundreds.

Barbara Gitlings, a Philadelphia librarian and lesbian, says, "What the homosexual wants—and here he is neither willing to compromise nor morally required to compromise—is acceptance of homosexuality as a way of life, fully on par with heterosexuality."[1]

This sentiment reflects a less harsh position reported by the Committee on Public Health of the New York Academy of Medicine in 1964. The report, the first authoritative study of homosexuality by a recognized organization representing all branches of medicine, states, "They would have it believed that homosexuality is not just an acceptable way of life but rather a desirable, noble, preferrable way of life. For one thing, they claim that it is the perfect answer to the problem of the population explosion."

The Rev. Robert W. Wood, a United Church of Christ minister, is even more emphatic. He says that homosexuality is a "God-created way of protecting the human race on this planet from the suicide of over-population,"[2] and that we should "pause to give thanks for the presence of homosexuality and its adverse affect on the birth rate."[3] According to this minister the all-knowing deity devised homosexuality "to permit sexual expression without a corresponding increase in population.''[4]

If this is the goal why not legalize bestiality? As Max Rafferty, former Superintendent of Education in California, put it: "The suggestion that the best way to curb Mr. Stork is to raise a generation of sex perverts is as outrageously false as it morally monstrous."[5]

History records many illustrations of homosexual activity (the Spartans, for example, practiced the concept that homosexuals were made and encouraged all male warriors to engage in homosexual liaisons), but today we are being bombarded with homosexual demands nearly unprecedented in history.

According to the 1972 Gay Rights Platform homosexuals are seeking the following course of action: amend the federal Civil Rights Act to prohibit discrimination against homosexuals in employment, housing, public accommodations and public services; a Presidential executive order prohibiting the military from excluding homosexuals; a Presidential executive order prohibiting discrimination against homosexuals in security clearances; allow homosexual aliens into the country; federal support for sex education courses presenting homosexuality as a valid, healthy preference and lifestyle as a viable alternative to heterosexuality; federal funding of homosexual organizations; the release of homosexuals from prison who were convicted because of sex offenses; repeal of all state laws prohibiting private sexual acts involving consenting persons (not adults); repeal of all state laws prohibiting solicitation for private voluntary sexual liaisons and laws prohibiting prostitution, both male and female.

The 1972 Platform also demanded enactment of legislation so that child custody, adoption, visitation rights, fostering parents and the like shall not be denied because of sexual orientation or marital status. It asked for repeal of all laws prohibiting transvestism and cross dressing and the repeal of all laws governing the age of sexual consent.

These are just some of the stated goals of the gay liberation movement. According to *Time* magazine, homosexuals are pushing hard for the same legal rights that society accords married couples.[7] For example, the San Francisco Board of Supervisors voted to recognize the live-in lovers of homosexual city workers as dependents entitled to the same health care benefits as heterosexual spouses. The Board voted 8-3 in favor of the measure only to have Mayor Dianne Feinstein veto it, not because of the radical live-in lovers concept, but because she considered it "inequitable."

In other words, the homosexual revolution is demanding full human and civil rights on par with heterosexual rights. If a heterosexual can adopt children, a homosexual must also be permitted to do so. If a heterosexual can head the CIA, a homosexual can also do so. If a heterosexual spouse can obtain health benefits, so must a homosexual live-in lover. There is to be no discrimination of any kind based on sexual orientation in spite of the fact that "no state in the Union officially recognizes gay marriages."[8]

The mass media, of course, makes it easy to feel such activity is unprecedented, and observers of the homosexual sub-culture concede that a real homosexual move is underfoot, and that its power is more pervasive than most wish to admit. One example of such power is given in TV producer James Komack's statement, "Do you know the most powerful lobby in the entertainment business? Bigger than Blacks or women's lib or any nationalist or racist group. It's the gays. If you don't have the approval of the Gay Media Task Force, you don't go on the air."[9]

The head of the Gay Media Task Force is Newton

Deiter. "These days," says *TV Guide,* "The three networks send Deiter virtually all scripts involving 'gay themes'." [10] Deiter seeks to make sure the one acting the homosexual role "has the kind of boy-next-door good looks and mannerisms" that "physically he's tall, all American." He also insures that certain expressions are deleted and is not hesitant to sprinkle the script with the note: "The Young Gay Man is NOT effeminate." [11]

*TV Guide* refers to Deiter and his "agents in place" (meaning homosexuals in the entertainment industry) as "the Gay Mafia". The basic goal of the Gay Mafia is to guarantee "positive portrayals of homosexual characters and themes" on television and in the movies. Witnessing such works as "Love, Sidney," "A Question of Love," "In the Glitter Palace," Dynasty's portrayal of Steven Carrington, "That Certain Summer," "Soap," "Making Love," "Partners," "Victor-Victoria," "Sergeant Matlovich vs. the U.S. Air Force," "The Naked Civil Servant," "The War Widow," "Car Wash," "Next Stop, Greenwich Village," etc. may lead one to accept James Komack's conclusion. Certainly the Gay Mafia is extremely powerful.

## In The Classroom

Homosexuals want teaching positions, as the classrooms provide excellent recruiting grounds. More than ten years ago the *Miami Herald* (April 12, 1966) issued a warning stating, "Innocent youngsters and apathetic parents are a dangerous combination. One of the major recruitment systems operates within the school."

A dirty sex joke in class, an invitation home, drugs, alcohol, dirty pictures and sex talk make potent recruiting weapons. To read accounts, such as the following, "Orange County High School band director was charged with ten counts of disgusting sexual relations with boys under eighteen years of age..." is becoming more and more commonplace. And if state and federal laws give homosexuals free access to the classroom, these incidents will become legion.

Right now, for example, public schools in San Francisco, ostensibly the gay capital of the world, teach school children "greater respect" for homosexual lifestyles. The school board set up a new program on the advice and request of the local Gay Advisory Committee, and, sadly but interestingly, it appears that federal money (our tax money) is being used to finance the program.

Commenting on such a program Dr. Max Rafferty said, "When you teach little children all about the ins and outs of an abomination of this sort, you're instilling in their minds that this sort of thing must really be all right or they wouldn't be teaching it in school." [12]

## Is Homosexuality Normal

The question before our nation is whether or not homosexuality should be considered normal sexual behavior.

If the answer is "yes," then obviously homosexual life-styles should be presented to our nation's youth as normal. Such activity already is prevalent in many schools, colleges and universities, but it is kept on the quiet side. One can hardly imagine what the situation would be like if the "closet" activity were to become public.

However, there are good and sufficient reasons why homosexual activity should not be considered normal.

Scripture makes it exceeding clear that homosexuality is a mark of social decline. History records that the Greek, Roman, Persian and Moslem civilizations declined as homosexuality became more prevalent within those cultures. Homosexuals have a tendency to turn against their parent society if it does not succumb to

26

homosexuality. They will subvert their own nation if they consider it to be too moral or anti-homosexual.

The American public must make its decision: Will America maintain a Biblical value system and move toward moral health and restoration, or will She follow other civilizations on the road to paganism and decay? The Marxist historian, Alfred Leslie Rowse, observed in his work, *Homosexuals in History* (1977), that America "sprang out of the bosom of the repressed (and repressive) Puritans. Therefore, it "is to be expected that Americans are hag-ridden by Puritan conscience" and "Christian repressions" toward homosexuality, but in the "revolutions of our time, the breakdown of religion, conventions, the transformation of social and moral structures, men are free to realize themselves and their own natures as they are."

The patent homosexual argument is that "new" Biblical insights and modern psychology and sociology have given rise to a new interpretation and appreciation of homosexuality; however, others have observed that one need not be a Ph.D. to know that when some forty-year-old male paints his face with rouge and lipstick and prances around in women's clothes, "He ain't playing with a full deck." We agree. We believe that so-called "new insights" cannot change the natural order created by God. In fact, the so-called "new" Biblical insights are merely the "old" liberal higher criticism of the 19th century. And if modern psychology and sociology are used to bolster the homosexual case, their awkward defense serves only to reveal the bankruptcy of "modern" psychology and sociology.

If sociologists, psychologists and theologians voted tomorrow to consider as normal transvestism, fetishism, voyeurism, pedophilia, exhibitionism, necrophilism, masochism, bestiality and incest, their vote still would not make such desires or practices "normal". Such a vote, however, would give us great insight into the nature of those "new" scholars!

Homosexuality, masochism, bestiality and incest have not changed from what they were thousands of years ago. God condemned such activity then and He condemns it today. "Modern" thought might try to make such behavior respectable, but again, such an attempt merely manifests the bankruptcy of "modern" thought. It does not change the unnatural activity of those practicing such behavior. Fortunately, approbation of such deviant behavior is by no means universal; many modern thinkers feel that homosexuality is still a perversion and a present danger to society.

Although homosexuals and the pro-homosexual media are stone-silent about the seduction of the young, it is no secret that such activity plays a significant part in their irrational world. Magazines and newspapers, for example, which cater to homosexuals feature pictures of nude boys as young as ten and eleven years of age. As one homosexual put it, "In all sexuality, even heterosexuality, the younger sex objects are the most attractive." [13]

Homosexual propaganda wants the non-homosexual community to consider child seduction and molesting an old stereotyped view of homosexual activity. Nothing could be further from the truth for pederasty has always been a constant fixture in pro-homosexual literature.

The homosexual community has consistently called for the lowering of the age of sexual consent. Some want it as low as 13 years of age. Others to 4 years of age (Rene Guyon Society) and still others want no age limits whatsoever.

To protect one's sons and daughters from such influence should be the minimum parental responsibility—especially when one reads that "the natural history of

28

the homosexual person seems to be one of frigidity, impotence, broken personal relationships, psychosomatic disorders, alcoholism, paranoid psychosis, and suicide."[14]

A.L. Rowse, an Oxford professor, may castigate Christianity and Puritanism and even glorify homosexuality, but he also has to record the fact that many of his favorite homosexuals committed suicide. And even today, fifty percent of all suicides and homicides in big cities can be attributed to homosexuality.[15] What parent would want such a life and death for his child?

Non-homosexuals have rights, too—and when there is a conflict of rights, we must turn to the Creator from whom all human rights issue. God ordained the male/female family unit just as He ordained both Church and State. It is inconsistent at best for homosexuals to advocate that one God-ordained institution, the State, should be used to weaken or destroy yet another of God's institutions, the Family. Indeed, under our system of government, the State derives its power from the consent of those governed—all of whom are products of male/female families. Scripture, nature and common sense show that heterosexuality is the only natural sexual norm.[16]

## The Homosexual Threat

Recently, a well-known United States psychiatrist, Dr. Shirley Van Ferney, warned that the homosexual movement sweeping the country is a "threat to the nation's children." Because the threat is mounting, Dr. Van Ferney, a member of the psychiatric staff at New Jersey's Medical Center in Princeton, urged parents to fight it.

In 1977 Dr. Van Ferney said that "constant media coverage of the gays has made their life-style appear to be commonplace and acceptable rather than unusual and deviant.

"Parents are absolutely correct to be fearful of the effects all of this is having on their kids," she added. "Homosexuals are so active on high school and college campuses that there is hardly a child in America who has not been exposed to their influence.

"Parents must take a stand for their rights or they stand to lose these rights," she said. "You have a right to raise decent children in a decent society," she told reporter Maury M. Beecher, "but that right will be taken away from you unless you make yourself heard. If parents capitulate to the homosexual influences which surround them, society as we know it will be destroyed." [17]

Psychiatrists Dr. Samuel Silverman and Dr. Charles W. Socarides, and psychologist Dr. Frank M. duMas, agree that homosexuals are after the young:

Dr. Samuel Silverman, associate professor of psychiatry at Harvard Medical School, said, "I would also advise parents to protest vigorously if any of their children's teachers are professed homosexuals.

"It's very admirable to be tolerant and sensitive to people's civil rights—but you have to draw the line somewhere, and a homosexual teacher who flaunts his sexual aberrations publicly is as dangerous to children as one of the religious cultists.

"Homosexuals have not only come out of the closet, they have become militant. They are demanding all kinds of 'rights'...to be fully accepted as 'normal,' to be able to marry, to adopt and raise children and to have their life-style presented as a perfectly normal alternative to heterosexuality.

"Many of these militant gays are not fighting for their own civil rights but are attempting to win converts to their way of life."

Dr. Silverman added: "What is really needed now is a ground-roots movement against these militants."[18]

Dr. Charles W. Socarides, clinical professor of psychiatry at the State University of New York and a leading authority on the treatment of homosexuality, warned:

"There's no doubt in my mind that if homosexuality is further normalized and raised to a level of complete social acceptability, there will be a tremendous rise in the incidence of homosexuality. It would have dire effects for society. Homosexuality militates against the family, drives the sexes in opposite directions and neglects the child's growth and sexual identity."[19]

And Dr. Frank M. duMas, professor of psychology for 25 years, says that "homosexuals have repeatedly approached" his four boys and are a menace to society. "In the last twenty years," he says, "homosexual activists have achieved amazing political success in obscuring the issues, derogating thousands of years of human experience and research on the subject of and changing attitudes in the general population."[20]

1. *Time,* September 8, 1975, p. 43.

2. Edward Batchelor, Jr., editor, *Homosexuality and Ethics* (New York: The Pilgrim Press, 1982), p. 165.

3. *Ibid,* p. 166.

4. *Ibid.*

5. *Kappan,* October, 1977, p. 91.

6. The 1972 Gay Rights Platform is reprinted in whole in Enrique T. Rueda, *The Homosexual Network* (Old Greenwich, Conn.: The Devin Adair Company, 1982), p. 202f.

7. *Time,* December 13, 1982, p. 74.

8. *Ibid.*

9. Anita Bryant, *The Anita Bryant Story* (Old Tappan, New Jersey: Fleming A. Revell Company, 1977), p. 103.

10. *T. V. Guide,* May 30, 1981, p. 3

11. *Ibid,* June 6, 1981, p. 50.

12. *National Enquirer,* June 28, 1977, p. 5.

13. Reported in John W. Drakeford, *A Christian View of Homosexuality,* p. 98.

14. Daniel Cappon, *Toward an Understanding of Homosexuality* (Englewood Cliffs, New Jersey: Prentice Hall, Inc., 1965), p. 115.

15. *The Anita Bryant Story,* p. 96.

16. See George F. Gilder, *Sexual Suicide* (New York: Bantam Books, 1975) for a defense of the male/female family unit.

17. *National Enquirer,* June 7, 1977.

18. *Ibid.*

19. *Ibid.*

20. Frank M. duMas, *Gay Is Not Good* (Nashville: Thomas Nelson Publisher, 1979), p. xi.

Chapter 1

# The Homosexual Issue

*"The ordination of an avowed lesbian as a deacon in the Church is a sign of a healthy change."*

*—Right Rev. Paul Moore, Jr.*

Many Christians were awakened out of their moral slumber when in March, 1975, in Boulder, Colorado, two homosexuals were granted a marriage license. The two men, both twenty-seven years old, were denied a license in El Paso County but found the "moral" and legal climate more acceptable in Boulder.

Both were married in a religious ceremony October 28, 1973, at the Faith Metropolitan Community Church in Colorado Springs, Colorado.

Since that time, the homosexual issue has continued to occupy more and more print. One can hardly read a paper or a magazine without running headlong into the issue.

The Church is deeply involved. Government is involved. Schools are involved. Private and public organizations are involved. In short, each one of us is involved, whether we realize it or not. Homosexuality, for all intents and purposes, is fast becoming America's number one social issue, with from two to twenty million homosexuals involved. Moreover, as is true with all social issues, it has momentous religious and political implications.

To grasp the pervascence of the present homosexual revolution, observe the following items taken from the public media (*New York Times, Time,* Associated

Press, *Los Angeles Times,* United Press International, etc.)—all involving the major social structures of the nation:

## Homosexuals Petition F.C.C.

The Federal Communications Commission is being asked to extend the broadcast fairness doctrine to let homosexuals appear on television to counter criticisms of their life-styles...the petition was submitted by the Council on Religion and the Homosexual, Inc. June 17, 1977.

A committee appointed by the Catholic Theological Society of America is offering Catholics a new sexual morality. It is morality with no "yes" and "no" answers. Homosexual behavior is not to be condemned where it fosters personality growth. May 28, 1977.

The Anglican Church's attitude toward homosexuality may have to be altered in the light of 20th century knowledge, according to Bishop John Yates of Gloucester. Dr. Norman Pittinger, a theologian who admitted his own homosexual bias, claimed that Christian tradition was mistaken. He said a right understanding of love was essential. May 9, 1977.

The General Assembly of the Christian Church (Disciples of Christ) approved a resolution supporting laws to protect the civil liberties of homosexuals. Passed by a vote of 2,541 to 1,312 with 65 abstentions, the resolution calls for laws to "end the denial of civil rights and the violation of civil liberties for reasons of sexual orientation or preference." Oct. 25, 1977.

Saying it's time for frankness, a task force for the Ohio Diocese of the Episcopal Church has called for church acceptance of homosexual marriages and admission of homosexuals into the priesthood. The task force, which included three priests, a psychologist and a physician, said that by refusing to accept homosexuality the church forces celibacy on homosexuals it ordains without knowing of their homosexuality. Last year, the Episcopal Church's General Convention said homosexuals are children of God who have a full and equal claim with all other persons upon the love, acceptance and pastoral concern and care of the church. And Bishop Paul Moore of New York ordained an avowed lesbian last year. Sept. 28, 1977.

A homosexual ring operating from a Boy Scout troop may have victimized hundreds of boys and traded them like cards to other men. Sept. 12, 1976.

## Homosexual Slave Market

Gay community leaders complained today about the arrest of 40 persons in what police called a sado-masochistic slave market. Captain Jack Wilson said the building in which the auction took place was equipped with dungeons and cell blocks. In the dungeons were all forms of chains and articles of restraint. Mark IV club was maintained by a group calling itself "the Leather Fraternity" as a private club for homosexuals and sadomasochism cultists. April 14, 1976.

"In all, I guess there were between 25 and 30 boys killed, and they were buried in three different places..." Henley told police that Corll had turned on him and two other youths, threatening to sexually molest and kill them. Henley said he had managed to kill Corll in self defense. He then recounted to Houston police an incredible tale of horror, homosexual sadism and mass murder. August 20, 1973.

They call themselves "chicken hawks" and they openly advertise in magazines for "chickens." The "hawks" are grown men...homosexuals. The "chickens" are boys, ages 10-14. The "hawks" want the "chickens" for sex. The "hawks" take pictures of themselves with the "chickens" and pass them around. It is a disgusting business. March 30, 1977.

Sexual abuse and exploitation of an estimated 30,000 children in the Los Angeles area—predominantly boys ages 6 to 17—has spurred a crackdown by juvenile officers of the Los Angeles Police Department. November 21, 1976.

Five men were charged Wednesday with 47 counts of sex acts with boys between the ages of 9 and 14...All charges stem from the investigation of the operation of an alleged homosexual ring involving now disbanded Boy Scout Troop 147. March 24, 1977.

A 15 year-old boy testified Wednesday that he engaged in homosexual acts with defrocked Episcopal priest Claudius I. "Bud" Vermilye. The boy buried his face in his hands and answered with muffled "yes" when prosecutors asked if Vermilye had performed the sex acts on him. June 6, 1977.

## Thousands of Gays March

Paul Hardman of the Pride Foundation, a moderate gay organization noted for its legal work on cases of discrimination against homosexuals, said, "We're asking everyone to be cool on Sunday (June 26, 1977), to keep a low profile. We expect 140,000 people to march here (San Francisco), but we don't want the agitators or the lunatic fringes." June 21, 1977.

Dallas police uncover nationwide homosexual procurement ring in raid on Dallas apartment...seize catalogue files containing names and addresses of 50,000 to 100,000 people around the country, booklets containing pictures and names of teenagers and young adult males, available through the ring for homosexual activities. August 16, 1973.

A 34 year-old bachelor Los Angeles elementary school teacher was arraigned on 16 felony counts involving alleged sexual relations with at least six of his present and former boy students...The investigation began last week after the mother of one young boy grew suspicious about her son's apparent emotional distress and quizzed him. The child finally told her about a sexual contact with the teacher. July 10, 1977.

More than 200 homosexual faculty members and graduate students meet at John Jay College and discuss methods of using professional abilities to combat myths of homosexuality; urge other homosexual college professors to declare their homosexuality and unite to end discrimination against homosexuals on campus. November 24, 1973.

Five hundred guests rocked the hall with applause, cheers and congratulations when Pat Montclaire married Terry Block at Glide Memorial United Methodist Church (San Francisco). The story did not exactly go into the society pages. One reason, perhaps, is that both bride and groom are males. November 25, 1971.

Fifteen men—including a mechanic, a psychiatrist and a former assistant headmaster of an exclusive boy's school—were arrested Thursday in what authorities called a ring where homosexuals from around the nation staged sordid parties with boys as young as 9. December 9, 1977.

## One Night Stands

The gay-church movement was begun in 1968 in Los Angeles by Troy D. Perry, Jr., a former Pentecostal preacher. He performs "Services of Holy Union" for couples of the same sex. He prefers long-term "monogamous relationships" but confesses his own love life has not been that exclusive ("God has a permissive will"). "I believe there can be loving experience, even in a one-night stand." January 31, 1975.

Jesuit priest, John J. McNeill, suggests that God had a divine purpose in so creating human nature that a certain percentage of human beings are homosexual. Rather than being a menace to the community in general and the family in particular, they have an important role to play in preserving and strengthening values. September 30, 1976.

Former New York City Health Services Administrator H.J. Brown, two weeks after publicly disclosing that he is homosexual, announces formation of a new national civil rights organization for homosexual men and women called National Gay Task Force. It is expected to act as clearing house and coordinator for some 850 other homosexual groups in the United States and to press for federal legislation outlawing discrimination against homosexuals and repealing sodomy laws. October 16, 1973.

Two men, acknowledged homosexuals, were arraigned on two counts of murder, and the police said the men may be responsible for at least twenty-six other murders. Ten bodies have been found so far. July 6, 1977.

A homosexual prostitution operation offering boys as young as eight is doing a brisk, nightly business in a Times Square penny arcade...! "We're only beginning to become aware of the scope of the problem," one police officer said. "We're not against homosexuality—we're against children getting hurt." April, 1976.

## Homosexuals Attack Children

Homosexual attacks on children are sharply increasing, unleashing a whirlwind of tragedy that sometimes ends in the murder of young victims, police warn. Lured by adults, kids are turned into homosexuals, recruited for male prostitution and sometimes killed out of fear they will tell parents. "I have actually seen homosexuals recruit young boys," said Sgt. Herman Clark of the Flint, Michigan police juvenile bureau. "It's a fact of life. Let's tell it like it is." June 28, 1977.

The Episcopal bishop of New York, the Right Rev. Paul Moore, Jr., says that many clergymen in his Church have been homosexuals, and that the ordination of an avowed lesbian as a Deacon in the church is a sign of a healthy change. December 27, 1975.

One study taken by a homosexual group says the clergy heads the list in percentage of homosexual members, with businessmen second and actors third. August 26, 1976.

The governing board of the National Council of Churches is urging its members to work for the civil rights of homosexuals. By an 84-17 vote the board put homosexuality in the same category as race, sex, class, creed and place of origin as a distinction that breeds discrimination. March 7, 1975.

At a lavish ranch outside Austin, Texas, last spring, some 300 ranchers, bankers, oilmen and politicians drank, ate barbecue, smoked pot and paired off for lovemaking. The only unusual aspect of the weekend-long party was that the guests were homosexuals. September 8, 1975.

There are now some 4,000 gay bars in the country. The gay bar is usually a sexual marketplace. There are bars for writers, artists, blacks, collegians, business-men, middle-class women, drag queens, transsexuals, male prostitutes and sadomasochists. September 8, 1975.

Silver-glittered bodies, braless women in T-shirts and bronze-chested men in jeans turned out Sunday for the annual Gay Freedom Day parade, perhaps the country's strongest showing for the rights of homosex-uals. Police estimated the crowd size at about 240,000. June 26, 1978.

Crazed young perverts and middle-aged degenerates openly fondled each other in public—even kissing each other's bare buttocks, to the delight of the cheering on-lookers. This outrageous public exhibition of perver-sion last June 28 (1980) was only part of the sickening spectacle known as Gay Freedom Day in San Francisco —an annual parade of hairy homosexuals and leather-clad lesbians. Parade founder, Robert Humphries said, "The parade is the gay community for all the world to see and if the world doesn't like what it sees, it can damn well look the other way, because we are

beautiful, we are real and we are not going away."
July, 1980.

New York's mayor, Ed Koch, has already collided with the firemen's union on the sensitive issue of permitting homosexuals in the fire department. January 4, 1978.

The Unitarian Universalist Association has resolved to promote the hiring of openly homosexual and bisexual persons to leadership positions within the denomination and its local congregation. August 8, 1980.

Bishops of the Anglican Church of Canada will begin permitting homosexuals to be ordained as priests...The candidate's sexual preferences will remain a private matter between the candidate and his bishop. February 25, 1979.

Last month (Dec. 1982), police raided a NAMBLA "safe house" in Wareham, Mass., and found four boys, including Harold Baker, a 17 year-old who had been involved since he was 8 with Martin Swithinbank. Swithinbank, another Harvard-educated NAMBLA member, was sentenced to up to 75 years in prison last year after pleading guilty to charges that he used his Long Island home to have sex with boys ages 8 to 15... Pederasts prey on boys from deprived families coaxing them into sex by showing the boys photographs of man-boy sex to wear down their resistance. Pederasts often are interested in boys of a certain age only. Once the boys grow older, the men will end the relationship, sometimes passing them on to pederasts who prefer boys of the older age.. The cornerstone of NAMBLA's cause is summed up in one of its pamphlets: "Children should be treated like full human beings, not as the private property of their parents and the state." January 18, 1983.

The Third Lesbian and Gay Seminarians Conference has been scheduled for March 28 and 29, 1980, at Union Theological Seminary in New York City. January, 1980.

The promiscuous homosexual male has long been vulnerable to hepatitis and venereal diseases like syphilis and gonorrhea. But an unusual assortment of disorders—some of them deadly—has recently broken out in the homosexual community...The epidemic does not affect homosexual women; it seems closely linked to the life-style of gay men with many sexual contacts. It coincides with the burgeoning of bath-houses, gay bars and bookstores, etc. December 21, 1981.

Doctors alerted to unusually high incidence of some cancers among homosexuals have found outbreaks of two additional types of tumors among homosexuals in San Francisco. Dr. John L. Ziegler of the University of California Medical Center in San Francisco said that doctors at a clinic dealing with homosexuals have uncovered four cases of rare Burkitt's lymphoma and three incidences of squamous carcinoma of the tongue. March 31, 1982.

The survival rate after two years of AIDS: less than 20%. The bad news: "We are at the horizon of a new epidemic, rather than at the peak," says Dr. James Curran. "We are no longer acting like a quick solution is just around the corner. This epidemic will be with us the rest of our lives." The big question in AIDS (Acquired Immune Deficiency Syndrome) is who will be affected next. So far, the disease has mostly stricken homosexual men (72% of all cases). But a majority of the experts believe that what was once known as the "gay plague" will enter the general population... The most widely feared route into the general public is through blood transfusions. March 28, 1983.

Many researchers believe that a history of multiple venereal diseases and other infections plays a role in suppressing the immune system. Such a history is characteristic of sexually active gay men and may help explain why they are prone to AIDS... Alarmed by the association of AIDS with promiscuity, many homosexuals are radically altering their life-style; some are even turning to celibacy. March 24, 1983.

AIDS victims fall into four general groups (with some overlapping); 75% are homosexual men. Most are Caucasians in their 30s and 40s with a college education, incomes averaging $20,000, a history of prior infection with mononucleosis and venereal disease, and a sex life that has included many partners, more than 500 in several cases... It is hard to find anything positive in a deadly plague, but immunologists, virologists and cancer experts agree that AIDS represents a remarkable experiment of nature. September 6, 1982.

The New York based National Hemophilia Foundation has just called for a ban on homosexual and other high-risk blood donors, prompting the Coalition for Human Rights in San Francisco to condemn the move, comparing it to "miscegenation blood laws dividing black blood from white". In Los Angeles, meanwhile, Alpha Therapeutic Corp., which manufactures plasma products, says it will buy no more plasma from blood banks unless donors declare in writing that they are not male homosexuals, Haitians or needle-using drug addicts. February 14, 1983.

The nightclub Tracks is hardly a place where one would expect to find a candidate for mayor.

The discotheque—off the 20th Street Viaduct—is tricky to find. On weekend nights, when the crowds are the biggest, the parking is lousy. And, Tracks is a homosexual bar, one of the most popular in Denver.

But Federico Pena has been there. So have two other mayoral candidates, Wellington Webb and Steve Schweitzberger.

Courting Denver's homosexual vote may be of little significance in terms of political support.

No one is certain how many gay men and women are registered to vote, or how many might cast ballots in the May 17 election. No one is sure of even how many homosexuals live in Denver—although one guess is about 50,000.

"I think we can make a difference," Webb said, analyzing the impact of the homosexual vote.

Candidates in Denver did not always feel that way.

"The difference is that four years ago, we went to ask them their position on the issues." says Bill Olson, organizer of the futile "dump McNichols" campaign in 1979 and a supporter of Tooley this time around.

"This year, they are coming to us," adds the 45 year-old Olson, a businessman and gay activist. March 20, 1983.

And thus it goes . . . on and on. Pages seemingly out of Genesis 19. The names change, but the activity remains the same. Sodom and Gomorrah are apparently alive and well.

Certainly the time has come to recognize that the liberated homosexual movement represents an evil lifestyle which not only devours its own, but contaminates the non-homosexual community, as well.

Although realizing that all mankind is under the judgment of God, it should also be clear that no other sin of human nature is glorified as persistently as the sin of homosexuality. There are no Adultery or Fornication Task Forces. There are hundreds of homosexual task forces and organizations.

Agreeing with Dr. Kenneth S. Kantzer that "like our God, we must learn to love the sinner while condemning his sin," and also agreeing with Scripture that "all have sinned and come short of the glory of God" it is imperative that we inform ourselves about the homosexual issue and stake our position. Beyond that, we can alert others to the growing homosexual menace, and finally, we can pray and help all homosexuals find deliverance from their sin through our Lord Jesus Christ.

Chapter 2

# The Homosexual Struggle

*"Any professor who honestly feels and teaches that homosexuality is a perversion is in for a very difficult time at many colleges and universities in the United States."*

—*Frank M. duMas*

On June 7, 1977, voters of Dade County, Florida, repealed by a 7 to 3 margin an ordinance that protected homosexuals from discrimination in housing, employment and public accommodations.

The ordinance rejected by voters mandated that private religious schools could not refuse to hire a prospective employee because he was a homosexual; nor could employers fire anyone because of his sexual preference. Those who did "discriminate" were subject to a $500 fine and/or sixty days in jail.

In short, the homosexuals had, through the threat of state-imposed penalties, denied non-homosexuals freedom of choice in choosing with whom they might wish to associate. School authorities actually could be jailed for following their conscience in seeking to protect children from homosexual influence.

Under the ordinance, private schools—both religious and secular—would have been forced to hire or to continue employing homosexual activists, even though the schools and the parents who sent their children to those schools held the deepest conviction that homosexuality was a perversion not to be sanctioned or propagated.

By a peculiarity of the Dade County Charter, the Metro Commission had no authority over the large public school population of the county. Therefore, "the new homosexual license would be applied solely to private and religious schools." [1]

But, even with the resolution of the vote in Miami, the homosexual issue had not faded away. Less than three weeks after the Miami vote, 50,000 homosexuals crammed New York's Fifth Avenue, sidewalk to sidewalk for almost 1½ miles, protesting the Miami vote. And in San Francisco, 125,000 homosexuals marched in the streets. Other record number gay marches took place in Chicago, Atlanta, Los Angeles, San Diego and Seattle.

Homosexuals have met with representatives of the American Civil Liberties Union, the League of Women Voters and the women's liberation movement to press for specific federal legislation to advance their cause. On October 9, 1982 the National Organization for Women (NOW) set its national goals at its convention in Indianapolis. First on the agenda was to organize a national conference on Lesbian Rights for 1984.

Soon the whole country could well be involved in the homosexual debate, because two bills pending in the United States Congress (S. 430 and H. R. 2624) would make homosexuality a national political issue. The Senate bill introduced by Senators Tsongas, Cranston, Packwood, Moynihan, and Kennedy is to prohibit employment discrimination "on the basis of sexual orientation." Such a law would immediately open the military, State Department, FBI and CIA to homosexuals. The bill defines "sexual orientation as male or female homosexuality, heterosexuality, and bisexuality by orientation or practice." It says nothing about "consenting adults."

At least H. R. 2624 defines "sexual orientation" as "male or female homosexuality, heterosexuality, and bisexuality by orientation or practice, by and between consenting adults." Earlier House bills (H. R. 2998 and

H.R. 5239) used the terms "person or persons" instead of adults which left the door open for homosexuals to prey on the young, as long as the young person is consenting.

The House bill was introduced April 19, 1983 and was sponsored by Mr. Weiss, Mr. Waxman, Mr. Lowry of Washington, Mr. AuCoin, Mr. Studds, Mr. Yates, Mr. Torricelli, Mr. Frank, Mr. Towns, Mr. Solarz, Mr. Fauntroy, Mr. Dellums, Mr. Clay, Mr. Miller of California, Mrs. Boxer, Mr. Sunia, Mrs. Schroeder, Mr. Dixon, Mr. Weaver, Mr. Garcia, Mr. Fazio, Mr. Morrison of Connecticut, Mr. Edwards of California, Mr. Berman, Mr. Bates, Mr. McKinney, Mr. Crockett, Mr. Mitchell, Mr. Edgar, Mr. Green, Mr. Levine of California, Mr. Roybal, Mr. Rangel, Mr. Kostmayer, Mr. Sabo, Mr. Stark, Mr. Dymally, Mrs. Collins, Mr. Bonior of Michigan, Mr. Fogietta, Mr. Sikorski, Mr. Wheat, Mr. Lehman of Florida, Mr. Stokes, Mr. Shannon, Mr. Barnes, Mr. Howard, Mr. Leland, Ms. Mikulski, Mr. Conyers, Mr. Borski, Mr. Richardson, Mr. Matusi, Mr. Panetta, Mr. Dicks, Mr. Coyne, Mr. Hoyer, Mr. Schumer and Mr. Gray.

One of the sponsors, Rep. Gerry Studds of Massachusetts, was actually censured by the House of Representatives for having had sexual relations with a 17 year-old male page and making advances to two others. The 46 year-old Democrat called his admission before the House that he is a homosexual "an affirmation of my fullness as a human being." Joseph Sobran saw it a little differently. He felt that by taking a congressional page to Portugal for a 2½ week fling, "has proven it possible to be a pederast and a Pecksniff at the same time."

Just a few years ago 25 Representatives signed a similar gay rights bill. This year the figure is over 60. Slowly but surely the gay plague advances politically.

The House bill seeks to add to the Civil Rights Act of 1964 the words "affectional or sexual orientation." The earlier bills (H.R. 2998 and H.R. 5239) used the expression "sexual preference" but "preference" implies the concept of sexual choice whereas "orientation" implies the concept of having no choice in the matter. However, the new bill (H.R. 2624) does state that sexual orientation means by orientation "or practice" which certainly seems to imply choice.

By amending the public education section of the 1964 Civil Rights Act, however, it would force public education facilities to hire homosexuals. In fact, there is good reason to believe that employers—both public and private—would be required by federal law to seek out and hire homosexuals in the areas of schools, hospitals and other institutions. Such action would not only politically and legally legitimize homosexuality, but it would lend it respectability as an alternate lifestyle with grave consequences.

In order to stem this tide of homosexual activism, concerned Americans are going to have to voice their opinions or such amendments will become law by default.

## Out Of The Closet

Overnight, homosexuality has mushroomed into a menacing abomination. Sodomites are rushing out of the closet—defiant, militant, organized—clamoring for human, family and civil "rights" and respectability.

According to the Associated Press of May 28, 1977, a tax-supported agency of the federal government has opened public housing to unmarried couples living together and to *homosexual couples* living together. The action "taken quietly" early in May, according to AP, is subject to the approval of local housing authorities, but HUD received "very little response to its new concept of the family."

Thus 1.5 million public housing apartments and 333,000 private housing units for which the federal government (your tax dollars) may pay rental subsidies are open to homosexual couples. A HUD family need consist only of "two or more persons (of either sex or the same sex) sharing residency whose income and resources are available to meet the family's needs and who are either related by blood, marriage or operation of law or have evidenced a stable family relationship."

When Priscilla Banks, the former HUD housing program specialist who wrote the new rules, said that this concept of the family is "very new," she made the understatement of the year! The federal government in a backhanded way has legitimized homosexual marriages.

San Francisco's board of supervisors actually voted to allow the city's employees to sign up their "lovers" for spouselike health benefits, and allowed $5,500 in survivor's death benefits to Scott Smith, former lover of Supervisor Harvey Milk, who was shot to death in 1978.

## "Gay" Sex Education

San Francisco's board of education unanimously approved inclusion of "gay" life-style studies in sex education classes.

An advisory board is recommending revisions to the already adopted sex education program. The idea is (1) to indoctrinate the children so that they no longer think of homosexuals in negative terms, and (2) to train them to refer to deviant persons not as homosexuals, queers, or sodomites, but as "gays."

Furthermore, while the board of education allowed the course to be taught primarily in high schools, the Gay Teachers Alliance has now succeeded in getting it approved for use from kindergarten through senior high school.

However, you can be sure that the children will not be told that the gay world is far from the "gayness" that its name implies. For example, Dr. John White (University of Manitoba) writes, "As your age advances your chance of loneliness increases. Young faces are fair, young bodies beautiful, young movements quick and eager. But who is attracted to a 'tired old fairy'?" [2]

And Murray Norris, in an article entitled "There is Nothing Gay About Homosexuality," writes, "One of the biggest problems with homosexuals is their own loneliness. In homosexuals' own publications, in the writings of psychiatrists who treat them, in the words of the ministers who try to help them, there is this constant repetition of the loneliness of the homosexual life.

"Whoever decided to call homosexuals 'gay' must have had a terrible sense of humor...." [3]

Incidentally, the term "gay" at one time was a euphemism for a prostitute. Usually it has carried the connotation of immorality and racy living. Its underground usage to denote homosexuality dates from about 1900 and came into common use in the 1950s.

## Conservative "Gays?"

In New York City, Dr. Ralph Blair, president of the Board of Trustees of "Evangelicals Concerned" an organization sympathetic to the gay liberation movement hiding within the framework of conservative Christianity, said that, contrary to what some people claim, he had "...not seen any evidence of conversion to heterosexuality on the part of a homosexual who accepts Christ as Savior."

When *Christianity Today* writer Tom Minnery told of homosexuals being converted to Christ and forsaking their homosexuality, Blair devoted the Spring 1981 issue of *Review* (an Evangelicals Concerned quarterly) criticising Minnery's article. Blair said Minnery was merely perpetuating hurtful falsehoods, viz., that homosexuals can actually change. It appears that changed homosexuals are a threat to the whole gay ideology and such information must be suppressed. When Minnery says, "the fact is, many people are experiencing deliverance from homosexuality. The evidence is too great to deny it." Such talk sends shudders throughout the whole homosexual movement. The homosexual movement is seeking to make homosexuality synonymous with being black or female. Changed homosexuals destroy such notions.

Blair's efforts are directed at getting Christian people "to stop bearing false witness against our homosexual neighbors" and getting "our eyes open to the good gay Christians around us." What Blair fails to tell the evangelical community is that gay "Christians" seduce the young just as much as gay non-Christians. Besides that, gay "Christians" have just as much trouble telling the truth as gay non-Christians. There indeed may be homosexual "Christians," but the Apostle Paul certainly identified such conduct as sin when he wrote, "Know ye not that the unrighteous shall not inherit the kingdom of God? Be not deceived: neither fornicators, nor idolaters, nor adulterers, nor effeminate, nor abusers of themselves with mankind . . . shall inherit the kingdom of God." (I Cor. 6:9, 10) One thing is certain: There are no "good gay Christians."

## Sodomy Laws Fall

*Newsweek* (October 25, 1976) reported that since 1961 eighteen states have eliminated sodomy laws that bar sexual acts between consenting adults. Communities as diverse as Amherst, Massachusetts, and Los Angeles have approved ordinances prohibiting job, credit and other discrimination on the basis of sexual preferences. Many corporations now have a policy of nondiscrimination on the basis of sexual orientation in hiring and promotion.

According to the ACLU's *The Rights of Gay People,* only eight states (instead of eighteen) have actually eliminated their sodomy laws: California, Colorado, Connecticut, Delaware, Hawaii, Illinois, Ohio and Oregon. Texas is presently without any law against sodomy.

The executive director of Minneapolis' Big Brothers testified that in 1974 the City of Minneapolis adopted an ordinance giving special privileges to homosexuals—using language identical to the controversial law repealed by voters in Miami, Florida.

Shortly after passage of the Minneapolis ordinance, a homosexual applied as a volunteer for Big Brothers, a charitable organization found in many United States communities (including greater Miami). For decades Big Brothers has encouraged *normal male volunteers* to provide fatherly or brotherly companionship for fatherless boys.

When Big Brothers realized it could not, under the Minneapolis ordinance, refuse to accept the homosexual volunteer, it decided that it would pass along to mothers seeking companionship for their sons the information that a particular volunteer was known to be a practicing homosexual.

The homosexual volunteer then complained that this passing along of information violated his civil rights—and the Minneapolis Department of Civil Rights agreed with the homosexual volunteer, even suggesting that Big Brothers should place special advertisements for homosexual volunteers in the area's "gay" publications. The result of giving homosexuals the protection of law inevitably leads to this type of madness. Such laws commit absurdities against other legitimate institutions. However, in all fairness to Big Brothers it should be noted that in other cities where they operate they do provide mothers with such vital information.

In our nation's capital gays are given credit with being a key element in the victory of Mayor Marion Barry, a black, over two other black candidates. Barry, the most liberal candidate, spent several years cultivating the support of Washington's gay voters.

It paid off handsomely on election day, when, according to the *Washington Post,* "more than 75% of those working on Barry's campaign telephone banks were homosexuals." A homosexual political analyst noted that in "20 of the 21 precincts where Barry won 50% or more of the vote, homosexuals make up 20% to 33% of voters."

Once in office, Barry not only appointed numerous homosexuals to city offices, but proclaimed "Gay Pride Weeks," paraded with homosexuals and spoke at their rallies. It is no secret that Washington's City Hall is in constant contact with the homosexual community, and it's in this context that Barry nearly delivered to the homosexuals on a platter everything their hearts were crying for as contained in D.C. Act 4-69. It was signed into law by Mayor Barry, only to be soundly defeated by the U.S. House of Representatives in 1982.

The Act was originally prepared by Councilman David Clarke (D-Ward 1). Clarke's bill would have legalized "kiddie sex" and incest (both homosexual and heterosexual, of course). When pressure mounted against Clarke's original act the revised act did the following: (1) it removed all sanctions against homosexual conduct in the D.C. area, (2) it legalized adultery, fornication and bestiality, (3) it legalized sexual advancement by a teacher against a teenager over 17 years of age as long as no force was used, (4) it reduced the penalties for forcible rape and (5) the Act allowed wives to bring charges against their husbands under a multitude of circumstances.

Following the defeat of D.C. Act 4-69 the *Washington Blade* newspaper admitted that the prohomosexual statute was a struggle between two rival lobbies—the Moral Majority and the Gay Rights National Lobby. Said the *Blade*: "The vote was also a setback for Washington's politically influential Gay community. Gay leaders had played a significant role in drafting the legislation and, with the cooperation of city officials, had quietly orchestrated the lobbying effort to save the legislation after it came under attack from Jerry Falwell's Moral Majority."[4]

Even though the Act was defeated by the House of Representatives, it should not be forgotten that for all intents and purposes, our nation's capital is still the prime breeding ground of the homosexual revolution, and by such homosexual action we can calculate just how far they plan to carry their liberation program.

## N.C.C. Pro-Gay

Interestingly, in 1975 the National Council of Churches voted to take homosexuality out of the category of male prostitution, child seducers and transvestites and to put it into the category of race, sex, class, creed and place of national origin. Thus, by a simple vote, the NCC declared evil to be good!

In his concern for the rights of inverts and perverts, Rev. G. William Sheek of the National Council of Churches denied the charge that homosexuals seek to recruit and seduce children. This denial is representative of a new low of willful blindness, even for the NCC. It flies in the face of what is so obviously and historically true. Since homosexuals cannot reproduce, they must recruit the young. In order to work their will and way on youths, homosexuals turn the beauty of normal sex into a nightmare.

Of importance to Christians is the fact that Sheek did not even bother to quote the Bible in defense of his statements. Instead, he turned to the work of a liberal theologian (possible homosexual) who claims that neither homosexual inclination nor the act excludes "one from the domain of God's gracious intention." Such theological linguese translates: "Sexual relationships between homosexual partners are sanctioned by God."

It is not surprising in this hour of apostasy to see religious leaders reinterpret and, thus, scorn God's Word. They presume to place their own moral preferences above the revelation of God. Instead of measuring their morality by God's Word, they judge God by their morality. As C.S. Lewis would say, "God is placed in the dock." Absolute moral judgments are declared dead.

Liberal theologians are presently espousing three main theses relative to homosexuality: (a) the so-called homosexual condition is according to the will of God, (b) God had a divine purpose in so creating human nature that a certain percentage of human beings are homosexual, and (c) there is the possibility of morally good homosexual relationships, and the love which unites the partners in such a relationship rather than alienating them from God can be judged as uniting them more closely with God and as mediating God's presence in our world. [5]

## Homosexuals Not Born

The first and third points, as we shall see, are patently false, and the point that homosexuals are born is, likewise, apparently unprovable. Homosexuals are not born; they are made. Homosexuality is a learned behavior. Older homosexuals seduce the next generation of homosexuals. There certainly is no mystery about it. The pattern is well established. Between the ages of eight and eighteen or even six and sixteen, a child is propositioned or seduced. If the child participates in the sexual behavior, he is on the way to becoming a practicing homosexual.

In one study investigating the question whether homosexual desires or homosexual behavior comes first, it was discovered that in a significant number of cases the subjects had their first homosexual experiences before they were conscious of any homosexual desires. Forty-three percent of the subjects had their first homosexual experiences before they were twelve years of age. [6]

Homosexuality is not a matter of genes and chromosomes. *Time* commented, "The only thing most experts agree on is the homosexuality is not a result of any kinky genes." [7] Dr. John White noted, "Once I experience it, the more fixed will the pattern become. What I do determines what I am just as much as what I am determines what I do." [8]

In an article entitled "Gays and Lesbians on Campus" *Newsweek* reported "For some women, more so than for men, homosexual relations are just an experimental phase. Some lesbians on campus were not homosexual when they came to college and may not be after they leave." [9] Others say they are lesbians for political reasons. "The most radical lesbians reject heterosexuality as the oppression of a male-dominated society and maintain that women who are not lesbians cannot be feminists." [10]

At a lesbian workshop, feminists were told that "Every woman has the right to decide whether she will be homosexual, heterosexual, or bisexual." [11]

Such statements lend no support to the concept that homosexuals are born that way.

Even Kinsey acknowledged that there is no need of "hypothesizing peculiar hormone factors that make certain individuals especially liable to engage in homosexual activity, and we know of no data which prove the existence of such hormonal factors. There is no sufficient data indicating that specific hereditary factors are involved." [12]

The homosexual struggle has begun. It will last until Jesus returns and solves it. In the meantime we must be about our Lord's work, which surely includes standing firm on Biblical moral absolutes.

1. *The Anita Bryant Story,* p. 24.

2. John White, *Eros Defiled* (Downers Grove, Illinois: InterVarsity Press, 1977), p. 120.

3. *The Anita Bryant Story,* p. 96, 97.

4. Enrique T. Rueda, *The Homosexual Network,* p. 454.

5. John J. McNeill, *The Church and the Homosexual* (Kansas City: Sheed Andrews and McMeel, Inc., 1976), pp. 193-196.

6. John W. Drakeford, *A Christian View of Homosexuality,* p. 47.

7. *Time,* October 31, 1969, p. 64.

8. *Eros Defiled,* p. 111.

9. *Newsweek,* April 5, 1982, p. 76.

10. *Ibid.*

11. *The Homosexual Network,* p. 221.

12. Alfred C. Kinsey, et. al., *Sexual Behavior in the Human Female* (Philadelphia: W. B. Saunders Co., 1953), p. 447. Even though Kinsey is correct concerning hereditary factors he is certainly incorrect in many other facts of the homosexual issue. For a refutation of Kinsey's H-scale continuum and other Kinsey presuppositions see Dr. Frank M. duMas, *Gay Is Not Good,* pp. 153-157, 274-281. According to duMas, "The Kinsey Reports have probably been responsible for more people turning to homosexuality than any other factor, except for efforts of the homosexuals themselves."

Chapter 3

## The Homosexual Life-Style

*"Show me a happy homosexual, and I'll show you a gay corpse..."*
—*The Boys in the Band*

The straight community does not comprehend the homosexual world. The Christian community comprehends it even less.

What Christian, for example, could imagine a church convention where the city sites of interest were the local gay bars and massage parlors.

Yet at the eighth general conference of the Universal Fellowship of Metropolitan Community Churches, held August 1-7, 1977, at the Cosmopolitan Hotel in Denver, Colorado, this was exactly the situation. Those participating in the convention were furnished maps, but, instead of directing the participants to the Denver mint or to the gold-domed capitol, the map directed the communicants to the local homosexual church, gay bars and massage parlors.

The communicants of the convention were also flooded with a bevy of pro-homosexual books including *Homosexuality in the Light of Biblical Languages and Culture* by Arthur, *An Evangelical Look at Homosexuality* by Ralph Blair, *Homosexuality and the Bible* by Norman Pittenger and *Homosexual Catholics: A Primer for Discussion*.

It certainly is an understatement to say that gay bar activities, gay bookstores, gay dances with the pancake make-up, and homosexual bathhouses with "orgy rooms" do not fall within most people's frame of reference. Indeed, most normal or straight people have a difficult time imagining various types of homosexuals and just what it is that homosexuals do.

For example, Rev. Enrique T. Rueda in his book *The Homosexual Network* has a section in his chapter on "The Homosexual Subculture" that describes homosexual behavior at their gay bars and bathhouses. He notes that all homosexual publications advertise the gay baths. Says Rueda, "The degree of promiscuity in the baths defies the imagination of those not familiar with homosexuality. From the point of view of traditional values, they are probably some of the most destructive and degrading institutions in America today." [1] *Newsweek* recently described the many liaisons "among gay men (that) take place in the anonymity of the bathhouses." [2] Speaking of the disease AIDS, *Newsweek* comments, "An infectious agent loose in the hothouse environment of a gay bath, where some men have as many as 10 anonymous sexual contacts in one night, would spread exponentially." [3] The baths usually contain smaller rooms where homosexuals get together for sex and larger rooms called "orgy rooms" where group sex is conducted. Pornographic films are usually part of the menu. Homosexual diseases abound.

Of course, there are some groups that work overtime at making sure everyone knows exactly what homosexuals do. At the Colorado Women's Conference of the International Women's Year held in Boulder, June 3, 1977, the women in attendence were greeted with books displaying such titles as *What Lesbians Do, Ask No Man Pardon, Liberating Masturbation* and *Dynamite Damsels,* a comic book for children.

Although it might come as a shock, it should be noted that the homosexual sub-culture language contains over 12,000 terms used by homosexuals to identify themselves and their needs. [4]

For example, to "cruise" is to go out looking for sex. A "nellie" is an effeminate fellow, and a "butch" is a virile one. Male gays who project or seek hypermasculinity often go to leather bars to pick up a partner for S. and M. (sadism and masochism) or for B. and D. (bondage and discipline).

According to *Time* magazine leather bars are making "an increasing visible subculture in the gay world." In fact, many of the S-M practices, says *Time,* "take place at the bars, including handcuffing, whipping or urinating on a masochistic patron." [5] *Time* quotes C.A. Tripp to the effect that such activity is relatively frequent in homosexuality because of the addictive effect of two males together." [6]

Effeminate gay males are called "twinkies," "sissies" or "queens," and "fag" and "faggots" are acceptable terms among homosexuals if no "straights" are present.

Among lesbians, a "butch," "dyke" or "bull dyke" is a mannish women who seeks a "femme"—a passive, dependent partner.

In some gay bars the men's costumes, with their coded signals, are so elaborate that even the pros are beginning to get confused. According to Fisher's *Gay Mystique,* on the East Coast keys worn dangling from a homosexual's belt over the left hip, for example, usually signal a desire for sadism. [7] But even then, homosexuals may stare at each other for twenty minutes trying to figure out what each is trying to communicate.

If the communicators finally decide it is S&M each is pursuing they'll probably want to enroll in one of San Francisco's S&M workshops. The city coroner actually holds workshops in the gay community on S&M Safety, or "how to engage in sado-masochistic sex without permanent damage." Since 10% of San Francisco's homicides result from S&M among homosexuals, the coroner explains how to tie up a "lover without cutting off his circulation."

## "Man to Man"

Not all homosexuals resort to cruising gay bars looking for sex. Some enroll in such programs as "Man to Man," an organization endorsed by the homosexual Mattachine Society of New York. "Man to Man" uses a highly sophisticated questionnaire and an IBM 360 computer to match homosexuals for contacts. In fact, each homosexual participant is promised fourteen new contacts a month, and "that's a heck of a lot better than most people do in bars or on the streets," or so says the ad. The Society's questionnaire was prepared by Dr. Franklin E. Kameny, a leading figure in homosexual circles.

Some authorities delineate six specific types of homosexuals: the blatant, the secret lifer, the desperate, the adjusted, the bisexual and the situational.

The blatant homosexual is the obvious lisping, limp-wristed individual who is a caricature of femininity. This type also includes the leather boys who advertise their sadomasochism by wearing leather jackets and chains. These stereotyped perverts are a distinct minority and probably represent only about 10% of all homosexuals.

The secret lifers constitute the majority of homosexuals. They are hidden from all but their gay friends and "lovers," many wearing wedding bands and having wives and children. They are experts at leading double lives and pass as "straights." They range across all classes, races and occupations and live in constant anxiety lest their straight colleagues, friends and families discover their hidden vice and shun them.

The desperate homosexual is one who frequents public toilets, massage parlors and Turkish bathhouses. Referring to the public toilets as "tea rooms," this type of homosexual is desperate for immediate sex. They may be married men concealing their need by making contacts as anonymously as possible, and many have a dozen or more partners in a single evening.

## The Bisexual

The bisexual usually is a married man hiding behind his wife's skirts. He tells his male "lovers" how little he loves his wife, saying, "She's more like a mother to me," and does his best to keep his male "lovers" from marrying. However, he enjoys sex with both males and females and usually has affairs with members of both sexes. But nearly all bisexuals are actually homosexuals who aren't willing to admit that they really are homosexuals.

The "adjusted" homosexuals are those who frequent gay bars, or pool parties, pick up a "lover" and try to settle down to a "conventional" gay marriage. Most gay marriages, however, are short-lived. "If inconstancy and infidelity plague the straight world," says Dr. John White, "they plague the gay world to a far greater degree."[9]

Lastly, the situational homosexual is one who engages in homosexual acts without any deep homosexual motivation. Perhaps the best example of this type would be men in prisons, where female sexual partners are not available. Of course, many situational homosexuals may become more conventional homosexuals once they are released from prison.

## Homosexual Activity

Homosexual activity and seduction techniques vary among homosexuals. Some homosexuals visit gay bars and pander with someone their own age. Others prey on young boys—finding them on the street, in youth organizations or in schools, colleges or churches. John Maynard Keynes, the British economist, was a connoisseur of young male children at Eton and Cambridge.[10]

A few years ago, the nation was shocked when it learned of the murders of twenty-seven teenage boys in Houston, Texas, by a homosexual named Dean Allen Corll. Corll enticed the boys into his apartment, handcuffed them to a specially constructed plywood board, sexually abused them, and finally, either strangled them or shot them with a .22-caliber pistol. He buried his victims in three mass graves.

In more recent times, John W. Gacy, Jr. was charged with the mass murder in Chicago of 33 young men and boys. Gacy buried most of his victims under his own house.

The all-time homosexual mass murderer was Gilles de Rais, a knight, former colleague of Joan of Arc, and a seducer and murderer of young boys. He was hanged and burned on the gallows in the city of Nantes in Brittany in 1440. He was charged with the deaths of 800 victims—all children, each one innocent, each one poor, each one despicably abused. According to the book, *Bluebeard: The Life and Crimes of Gilles de Rais,* by Leonard Wolf, Gilles or a henchman would recruit a lad of 10 or 12 and take him to one of Gilles' chateaux. There the boy was bathed, dressed, fed, cheered, caressed, raped, murdered, dismembered, burned in Gilles' massive fireplace and sometimes eaten by Gilles himself!

## Pederasty

Homosexual teachers in colleges and high schools use both sophisticated and crude methods of seduction. Some merely tell shady jokes and watch the reaction of students. If some boys respond favorably, they then are approached and asked to come home with the instructor where obscene pictures are passed out and sex talk ensues until the victim is trapped. In other situations the instructor simply announces he will be at a particular gay bar and invites all to join him for a bash. Perhaps he chooses to invite them to a drug party where the victims are seduced with pictures and talk, while natural inhibitions are weakened by drugs. Still others take the intellectual approach, quoting Walt Whitman's lines, "...of a youth who loves me and whom I love, silently approaching, and seating himself near me, that he may hold me by the hand..." or Plato's rather obvious ode to pederasty, "Through the nightly loving of boys, on arising, begins to see the true nature of beauty,"[11] and then asking for an explanation or interpretation.

Homosexual clergy use a variety of techniques, too, but have an advantage most homosexuals do not possess. As "men of the cloth," they catch most of their potential victims off-guard and cause them to easily fall for the massage routine, oriental parlor techniques, sex talk and/or other subtle variations. Many religious perverts try to convince their victims that David and Jonathan, Ruth and Naomi or Christ and John the Apostle were homosexuals.

Homosexuals usually are very defensive when it comes to the subject of seducing youth. "Pedophilia," says Newsweek, "is the touchiest of homosexual issues."[12] Yet the homosexual lexicon The Queen's Vernacular uses such figures of speech as chicken, chicken queen, chicken freak, chicken hawk. Few wish to talk about mature male homosexuals stalking adolescents, then skilfully initiating them into the homosexual world of impossible fantasies.

Nevertheless, J.C. Coleman in his work Abnormal Psychology and Modern Life lists early homosexual experiences as the main cause of later homosexuality. He found that half of adult homosexuals had been seduced by older homosexuals before the age of fourteen.

Despite this reluctance on the part of homosexuals to deal honestly with the straight world, among homosexuals the issue is clearly understood. Witness the fact that a national guide to the trade, Where the Boys Are, has sold 70,000 copies at five dollars each! Besides, Donald Webster Cory, a literate and widely published homosex-

73

ual, states that there are two almost universal and strong drives among male homosexuals: the desire for a young lover and a lover with a gigantic sex organ. [13]

As one homosexual put it, "The adult homosexual often finds something attractive about younger partners. They always appealed to me, and a teenage boy looked particularly attractive. I have noticed, too, that some magazines which cater to homosexuals feature pictures of nude boys as young as ten or eleven." [14]

The passion of man-boy love can be felt in such poems as "The Unyielding Youth" in which the boy in the poem, who refuses to be seduced by the adult male, is actually called "wicked" and "cruel." The poem reads,

> Horace composed an ode about a certain boy...
> Whose soft cheeks were full of delicious sweetness...
> His nose was perfect, his lips flame red, lovely his teeth...
> But this boy, so lovely and appealing,
> A torment to all who looked upon him,
> Was made by nature so cruel and unyielding
> That he would die rather then yield to love.
> Harsh and ungrateful, as if born of a tiger,
> He only laughed at the soft words of admirers,
> Laughed at their vain efforts,
> Laughed at the tears of a sighing lover,
> He laughed at those whom he himself was causing to perish.
> Surely he is wicked, cruel and wicked,
> Who by the viciousness of his character denies the beauty of his body
> A fair face should have a wholesome mind,
> Patient and not proud but yielding in this or that...
> This flesh so fair, so milky, so flawless,
> So healthy, so lovely, so glowing, so soft -
> The time will come when it is ugly and rough,
> When this youthful skin will become repulsive.
> So while you bloom, adopt a more becoming demeanor. [15]

Fisher, in his book *Gay Mystique*, admits that "facts do indicate that a small minority of the male homosexual population does prefer boys in their mid-teens or early adult years as sexual partners.[16]

Fisher, however, doubts that we should be concerned about this! He says some will be concerned, even considering such activity "the most monstrous depravity," but, says Fisher (a homosexual himself), this attitude merely reflects "our cultural biases."

"In ancient Greece," says Fisher, "a young man was expected to take an adolescent boy for his lover and provide him with moral (sic) education and training in athletic and military skills."[17]

What Fisher does not state is that ancient Greece was pagan! Most American do not want a pagan Greco-Roman America. They want a Biblical America.

The homosexual publication *Christopher Street* quotes Tom Reeves, a Harvard graduate and professor of history, to the effect that, "I first realized I was gay and developed the ability to love men of all ages. But then I realized that I loved boys especially and felt the highest degree of intimacy in relationships with teenagers."[18] He refers to his pederasty as his "second coming-out." Homosexuals who are sympathetic to man-boy relationships, reports *Christopher STreet,* say that pederasty "may well be to the eighties what 'Gay is Good' consciousness was to the seventies—the cutting edge of sexual liberation."[19]

Edmund White in his work *States of Desires: Travels in Gay America,* describes with sympathy an interview he conducted with a 36 year-old Boston man who met his 12 year-old lover when the boy was 9.[20]

Even now, for example, there is a move in England to make pedophilia legally and socially accepted. It seems that the Paedophile Information Exchange feels there is a "need in Britain for a group of those men and women who are sexually attracted to young people of seventeen and below."[21] The Exchange is seeking to lower the age of consent to cover this "need" to the age of four.[22]

Although we might consider such an organization at the bottom of the British social level it turns out that the Paedophile Information Exchange has "discreet support in some corners of Westminster."[23] And even though its head, Tom O'Carroll, was arrested and convicted for "corrupting public morals" (in court PIE was described as "sick and a force for evil...which attracted dirty-minded predators.") the British have yet to shut down the operation. On the contrary, O'Carroll's book *Paedophilia: The Radical Case* has been published in England and the United States and is presently being sold in homosexual bookstores throughout our country.

O'Carroll certainly speaks the language of gay liberation. He quickly acknowledges, "I am a paedophile,"[24] a "lover of boys,"[25] and one seeking to abolish all laws "against consensual acts between children and adults."[26] Although O'Carroll admits he is an atheist,[27] he says at times he wishes he did believe because he could "appeal to the idea that I have been made as I am as part of His Great Purpose, and my love made accordingly."[28]

Whatever else one may say about O'Carroll, it is obvious that his sexual orientation is pederasty and he certainly falls well within the philosophical defense of pederasty by Socrates, Plato and Aristotle. How our own politicians are going to deny his kind of particular homosexual "rights" under the gay rights bill of "sexual orientation" and the gay charge of being born with an innate love for children is fascinating to contemplate.

Another reason why the British have yet to clamp down on PIE is that its membership includes Roman Catholic and Anglican clergymen, and members of Parliament. PIE's membership also includes Americans, Australians and Frenchmen. Its most famous (or infamous) member was Sir Peter Hayman, a leading British diplomat and defense official. Operating under the code name "Peter Henderson," Hayman was deeply involved with child pornography and with other members of PIE. Since Hayman had held positions in the Ministry of Defense and NATO, it was thought best to expose him so that he couldn't be blackmailed to reveal state secrets. [29]

In case someone reading this might feel that no such activity would ever be considered in the United States, let me quickly remind you that the February 1972 convention platform of A National Coalition of Gay Organizations in Chicago called for "repeal of all laws governing the age of sexual consent," [30] and "repeal all state laws prohibiting private sexual acts involving consenting **persons.**" To make matters worse the U.S. Commission on Civil Rights 1977 report entitled "Sex Bias in the U.S. Code" recommended reducing the age of sexual consent to 12—a position enthusiastically endorsed by the National Coalition of Gay Organizations.

The best known pederast organization is the North American Man/Boy Love Association. According to the Chicago *Sun-Times,* NAMBLA is a New York based group that advocates and promotes sex between men and boys. Its philosophy is "Children should be treated like full human beings, not as the private property of their parents and the State," [31] and "Sexual liberation cannot be achieved without the liberation of children." [32] NAMBLA clearly sanitizes its systematic exploitation of the weak and immature by the powerful and disturbed within the language of free sexual expression and the children's rights movement.

Founded in 1978 at a church in Boston, the group consists of well-educated professionals (many of them graduates of Harvard) who see nothing wrong in seducing boys aged 8 to 15. As the *Sun-Times* reports, "Pederasts prey on boys from deprived families coaxing them into sex by showing the boys photographs of man-boy sex to wear down their resistance. Pederasts often are interested in boys of a certain age only. Once the boys grow older, the men will end the relationship, sometimes passing them on to pederasts who prefer boys of the older age." [33] *Time* is even more graphic, "Wherever chldren go, that's where pedophiles go." [34] Contacts are made at bus stations, amusement arcades, the school yards. After making contact and friends, "the seduction is frequently played out," says *Time,* "over a period of weeks or months." [35] The seducer begins testing responses "to see whether the child will retreat or go along with a conspiratorial relationship." [36]

Before you reach the hasty conclusion that the organization is an insignificant group you'll be surprised to learn that NAMBLA is a civil rights organization dedicated to broadening the freedom of children—to give them the right to choose to be sodomized legally—no matter what their age. As a civil rights organization it publishes three periodicals: The Bulletin, the NAMBLA News and the NAMBLA Journal. [37]

After some of NAMBLA's members were arrested for sodomy, some of the other homosexual organizations mildly slapped their wrists, but as Joseph Sobran notes: "The homosexual movement has shown no inclination to reject pedophilia in principle, and the pedophile movement has arisen within the homosexual movement." [38] He also said, "NAMBLA has mixed freely for years with the gay rights movement, placing articles and advertisements in the gay press and representatives in the gay marches. It also speaks fluently the language of gay ideology." [39] Even the *Gay Community News* notes, "The Gay Activists Alliance has held a position for several years in favor of abolishing all age of consent laws." [40]

Nevertheless, Virginia Apuzzo, executive director of the National Gay Task Force, says "the mainstream gay rights movement is essentially a movement to secure the rights of consenting adults, and I underscore adults." [41] What Virginia Apuzzo does not mention is that the 1972 Gay Rights Platform **doesn't mention adults!** It reads, "Repeal of all state laws prohibiting private sexual acts **involving consenting persons.**" [42] It also reads, "repeal all laws governing the age of sexual consent." [43]

Enrique T. Rueda summarizes the role of children in the gay liberation movement as follows: "Although not all active homosexuals seem to have or want to have relations with children, the existence of child-centered pornography ("kiddie" porn) and very young homosexual child prostitutes [some place the number at 300,000 boy prostitues [44] with a yearly income at $3 billion [45]], it is a clear indication that homosexual pedophilia (also called pederasty) is a widespread phenomenon." [46]

Perhaps the best example to prove that homosexuals have their eyes on our children is illustrated in the Washington, D.C. Act 4-69 that was stopped in its tracks by the U.S. House of Representatives. The pro-homosexual bill would have legalized "kiddie sex" and as one stated, "teen-aged sexual activity that is consensual is not an area for criminal law." [47]

Also, *Time* magazine is worried about an idea gaining currency within the sex establishment—"Very young children should be allowed, and perhaps encouraged, to conduct a full sex life without interference from parents and the law." [48] Mary S. Calderone, a leading spokeswoman of the Sex Information and Education Council of the United States (SIECUS), is quoted to the effect that the child has a fundamental right "to know about sexuality and to be sexual." Wardell Pomeroy is quoted as saying that incest "can sometimes be beneficial." But notes *Time,* "The fact that such views fall just short of a manifesto for child molesters' lib is not lost on pedophiles. Valid Davila of the Childhood Sensuality Circle …welcomes the new writing, 'We believe children should begin sex at birth.'" [49]

David Thorstad, a homosexual and militant spokesman for the pedophiliac movement, says he is fighting for "the rights of children to control their own bodies." [39] Remember, it was Thorstad who said elsewhere, "I think that pederasty should be given the stamp of approval. I think it's true that the boy-lovers are much better for their children than the parents are and at a minimum, it's something that doesn't harm the boy at all." [51] Child Psychiatrist Leon Eisenberg of Children's Memorial Hospital Medical Center, Boston, however, says that people who think small children are capable of making free decisions about sex with adults are "full of crap." [52]

Some homosexuals in England are boycotting homosexuals who are seeking to lower the age of sexual consent. But, as opponents have observed, "The natural question is on what grounds homosexuals may rationally discriminate against those of other 'sexual and affectional orientation.'" [53] Viewing the question from a logical moral base requires that one asks the question: If casual sex is licit and innocent, why draw the line at children? If indeed homosexuals have no sexual norms, how shall we recognize "normality"? Once we accept the "normality" of the act itself and the ideological declaration that "gay is good," the age of the participants involved becomes a moot issue. Our philosophical and moral base for argument no longer exists.

The pederasts usually seek philosophical support for their abomination by appealing to Plato's dialogues, especially *Symposium* or *The Banquet.* However, the Greek explanation for the origin of homosexuality ("In the beginning there were three sexes—male-male, female-male and male-female. Each individual was built like a cylinder, with a double head on one round neck and two faces pointing in opposite directions, etc."[54]) is as unreal and bizarre as the practice of pederasty itself.

Although Socrates (the world's most famous homosexual who was put to death for corrupting the morals of minors), Plato and even Aristotle spoke of pederasty (man-boy homosexual relationships) as a higher form of love than heterosexual love (the argument being that heterosexual love was based on sensual pleasure and childbearing while pederasty—an older man and a young boy (usually 13 years old)—was based on friendship and intellectual interaction) the myth of pederasty is a far cry from its reality.

As Dr. Frank M. duMas notes, the reality of pederasty (sometimes referred to as "Greek love") is essentially sodomy between an older man and an immature child between the ages of ten to twenty.[55]

However, even though it is not legal in this country to seduce the young, shocking information regarding criminal exploitation of young boys continues to make the public press. On November 21, 1976, the *Los Angeles Times* news service carried an article reporting, "Sexual abuse and exploitation of an estimated 30,000 children in the Los Angeles area—predominantly boys ages 6-17 —has spurred a crackdown by juvenile officers of the Los Angeles Police Department. Captain William J. Riddle, commander of the Juvenile Division, said a six-week investigation revealed that thousands of youthful victims are being subjected to every conceivable sex crime, including acts of sadomasochism.

"The figures are based on street estimates," Riddle said, "and information from victims, witnesses and suspected sex offenders show that virtually all geographic areas and segments of Los Angeles society are affected by the problem...Based on the preliminary investigation by the police, it is estimated that at least 2,000 local adult males actively pursue boys under the age of 14. More than 25,000 juveniles from 14 to 17 years of age are used sexually by approximately 15,000 adult males. Pornographic materials are shown to juveniles to stimulate them sexually and narcotics are used to lower their inhibitions.

"'This is not just a Los Angeles problem, although it is becoming more prevalent here,' Capt. Riddle said. 'It's like a contagious disease, similar to the contagion of narcotics abuse, and it's spreading all over the country.' Investigation into a nationwide prostitution ring, involving juvenile boys, uncovered in Chicago, revealed that many of the young victims had been recruited in Southern California." [36]

In other cities additional reports continue to emerge: "Seven men were arrested in October 1976, when New Orleans police broke up a homosexual ring operating in a Boy Scout troop through which hundreds of young boys were victimized and traded among older men. New Orleans police seized letters, computer questionnaires and files indicating the ring was a national clearing house for homosexuals seeking young partners. The ex-Scout leader finally received a forty-five-year sentence for crimes against nature." [57]

This type of homosexual activity is referred to in the trade as "chicken hawking." The "chicken" is the young victim, while the "hawk" is the adult male pervert. It is all part of the sickening homosexual life-style.

## Classroom Activity

A few years ago a California Board of Education member demanded an investigation into the appearance of two homosexuals at a sex education course in a San

Francisco suburban junior high school. Eugene Ragle of Roseville said that this incident, in addition to a similar incident which occurred in a class at Redwood High School in Larkspur, Marin County, California, was evidence of "injection of illicit sex instruction and perversion in some schools. Principal Walter Nolan of Redwood High School confirmed that homosexuals did appear in a class discussion.

The homosexuals were invited by teachers, with the knowledge of parents, according to Nolan. The adult homosexuals had appeared in about six of thirteen social studies classes when students started "needling" them. The visitors responded with "explosive language," and "a few obscenities were used." The visits, also held in three other schools, were then cancelled. "In a town like San Francisco, kids—**and especially boys**—need education in all kinds of sexual behavior," said Eugene Huber, director of family life planning for San Francisco schools.

The homosexuals have made further gains in the San Francisco area. The San Francisco School Board passed a resolution ordering a study of curriculum changes to help pupils understand and tolerate homosexuals. No opposition was voiced to the resolution proposed by the city's Human Rights Commission and introduced by board member Peter Mezey. The school board had endorsed a policy two years earlier which bars discrimination against homosexual teachers.

Such homosexual activity verifies exactly what *Time* magazine recorded back on Sept. 8, 1975. Said *Time*, "Many fear the demands that seem to flow logically from the assertion that 'gay is good,' for instance, homosexual instruction in school sex courses...and gay love stories to go with heterosexual puppy-love in libraries and schools. The Task Force on Gay Liberation of the American Library Association has already begun such a campaign.

One such tool the Task Force has available is a book by Morton Hunt entitled *Gay*. Published by Farrar, Straus and Giroux, the book describes in explicit detail the sexual acts of male and female homosexuals.

School librarians are being urged to purchase the 210 page book so that children twelve years old and older can learn about a "natural" practice (although perhaps not as natural as heterosexuality) and can be encouraged to know that there is a homosexual community where they will be made welcome.

Another cause for concern with the homosexual lifestyle lies in the fact that there seems to be some relationship between homosexuality, atheism, Satanism and nihilism.

In Romans, chapter one, the Apostle Paul describes how man first rejected God's planned order and finally rejected God. The homosexual has rejected God's planned order of male/female. From there it is but a short step to a total rejection of God. During Gay Pride Week, at a rally held in Boston, the speakers stood under a banner that read, "Christianity Is Our Enemy." One gay leader read from Leviticus and then burned the Bible. [58]

The world's most infamous sex pervert, the Marquis de Sade, has one of his characters declare, "My largest pleasure is to swear in God's name. My spirit abhors, scorns this disgusting fiction. I would like to discover some way better to revile it (God) or to outrage it further."

And one of de Sade's homosexual disciples put it even more bluntly: "The supreme evil, God."

A further cause for concern with the homosexual lifestyle is its tendency to spread venereal disease. The homosexual community is one vast reservoir of communicable diseases, including gonorrhea, syphilis, genital herpes, venereal warts, viral hepatitis (Types A.B. and

Non-A/Non-B), intestinal parasites (called the "gay bowel syndrome"), AIDS (Acquired Immune Deficiency Syndrome), Kaposi's sarcoma, Burkitt's lymphoma, Epstein-Barr virus and cytomegalovirus, among the more prevalent.

Dr. Paul Cameron summarizes the relationship between gays and their diseases as follows: (a) 49% of all syphilis in the U.S. is carried by gays, (b) 20% of all gonorrhea in the U.S. is carried by gays, (c) gays have a rate of infectious hepatitis eight to twenty-five times higher than heterosexual males, (d) two-thirds of gays have had at least one venereal disease, (e) in San Francisco over the past decade infectious hepatitis A increased over 100%, infectious hepatitis B increased 300%, amebic colon infection increased 2500%, the V.D. clinic saw 75,000 patients per year, of whom 70-80% were homosexual males, 20% of gays carried rectal gonorrhea, (f) homosexuality is associated with prostitution about 400 times more frequently for gays, and (g) bestiality is at least 300% more frequent among homosexuals than their heterosexual counterparts. [59]

Scientists are now warning the public of an epidemic caused by homosexuals that will affect the whole country. The question is, who will be affected next? "A majority of the experts," says *Time,* "believe that what was once known as the 'gay plague' will enter the general population." [60] And according to Dr. James Curron, director of the AIDS task force at the Center for Disease Control in Atlanta, "This epidemic will be with us the rest of our lives." [61] The Associated Press agrees, "AIDS will inevitably become epidemic throughout the nation." [62] What is not generally known, however, is that the homosexual disease now known as AIDS was originally termed GRID (Gay Related Immunodeficiency Disease). It was rechristened AIDS after lobbying by gay medical activists. These gay medicine men did not want the general public to perceive that "fast-lane" gays were the perpetrators of the disease upon the rest of society. With Hollywood and the media portraying homosexuals as the paragons of virtue such information could tarnish their image.

How did this insane situation come about? *Newsweek* explains: "The promiscuous homosexual male has long been vulnerable to hepatitis and venereal diseases like syphilis and gonorrhea. But an unusual assortment of disorders—some of the deadly—has recently broken out in the homosexual community."[63]

Elsewhere *Newsweek* states, "AIDS first struck extremely promiscuous 'fast-lane' gays. Many of the early victims had had more than 1,000 different sex partners, were frequent users of recreational drugs and had long histories of sexually transmitted diseases. The epidemic has now spread to include more conservative, even monogamous gays."[64]

"Among gays," says *Newsweek,* "sexual transmission of AIDS is almost a certainty."[65] In fact, the homosexuals themselves are having a difficult time coping with the fact that they "are dying of a gay related disease."[66] Instead of renouncing their sexual lifestyle, the gays are trying to convince themselves that their lifestyle is not sinful, AIDS is not a gay plague, and that God would not punish them for their promiscuous ways. Instead, the new gay slogan is "change your lifestyle, not your sexuality."[67]

In fact, it is even worse than that. When the gay physicians warned gay men to cut down on the number of sex partners, sex with strangers and sex acts that involved potential bloodletting (e.g., fisting) their warnings "were greeted with derision and charges of 'erotophobia.' "[68] To a certain vocal segment of the gay male community, "promiscuity in the face of AIDS," says *MS* magazine, "has consequently become a brave, even life-affirming stand against straight-style monogamy and sexual repression."[69]

According to Dr. Daniel C. Williams, a New York physician, the gay epidemic coincides with the burgeoning of gay bathhouses, gay bars and gay bookstores. He says, "The large number of anonymous contacts in gay bathhouses increases the risk of sexually transmitted diseases exponentially."[70]

Jeffrey Hart reports one homosexual as saying that casual promiscuous sex is essential to the homosexual ethos. Such sex, he says, takes place as casually as one might buy someone a drink. Hence, AIDS was damaging the entire lifestyle. Hart admits, however, that he did not know the average number of sexual partners for an active male homosexual is 1,600 during his active lifetime. "Nor had I known about the activities in the homosexual bathhouses, where I now learn, it is not unusual for a homosexual to have a dozen sexual encounters in the course of an evening. Or that homosexual bars feature a back room for the purpose of sex between strangers who meet at the bar." He concludes, "The behavior mentioned above does not indicate merely another 'sexual orientation.' It represents something entirely different from the behavior of heterosexuals."[71]

According to Dr. Frank duMas, "It is not uncommon for a homosexual person who performs fellatio to have a dozen different sex partners in one evening at a homosexual bath or toilet."[72] Dr. duMas further says, "Dozens of researchers have shown that homosexuals are as a group very promiscuous. For the largest group (male homosexuals), 60% had more than 250 sex partners and 28% had 1,000 or more sex partners."[73] This explains why San Francisco has a VD rate 22 times as high as the rest of the country. And Joseph Sobran certainly isn't wrong for stating, "Simply from the standpoint of public health, the community has a legitimate interest in discouraging homosexual activity."[74] Even some homosexuals may be having second thoughts. Randy Shilts, a San Francisco journalist ponders, "Isn't it something that what brought most of us here now leaves tens of thousands of us wondering whether that celebration ends in death."[75] And *Newsweek* seems to be wondering if gay is really good. "Ironically," says *Newsweek,* "the freedom, the promiscuity, the hypermasculity that many gays declared an integral part of their culture have come to haunt them."[76]

The situation has become so life threatening that the New York-based national Hemophilia Foundation has called for a ban on homosexual donors, and the Alpha Therapeutic Corporation will buy no more plasma from blood banks unless donors declare in writing they are not male homosexuals. Homosexual response? The Coalition for Human Rights in San Francisco condemned the move comparing it to "miscegenation blood laws dividing black from white."[77]

It appears that the American public is slowly waking up to the truth about the homosexual lifestyle. *Newsweek's* April 18, 1983 edition contains a cover story entitled "Epidemic" which exposes the medical threat of the gay community to the rest of the nation. The gay plague, says *Newsweek,* may be the "Public-Health threat of the century." The truth is that "the homosexual community is a medically diseased portion of the social body (and) their strictly physical ailments—most of them transmissible—are easily linked with the practice of homosexuality."[78]

*Newsweek* followed up their April 18th edition with another front cover story for August 8, 1983 entitled, "Gay America: Sex, Politics and the Impact of AIDS." Says *Newsweek,* "For Gay America, a decade of carefree sexual adventure, a headlong gambol on the far side of the human libido, has all but come to a close."

Some of the nation's best known homosexual bath-houses were closing because of the gay community's fear of promiscuous anonymous sex and the AIDS epidemic. *Newsweek* notes that there is hardly any doubt that AIDS is primarily communicated by homosexual male sex. The philosophy seemed to be "sex was liberating and more sex was more liberating." According to Dr. James Campbell of the University of California at San Francisco, "Anal intercourse theoretically provides an ideal opportunity for infection because the capillaries of the rectum are so close to the surface of the skin." *(Newsweek,* August 8, 1983, p. 40)

Instead of the gay leadership admitting the obvious, however, the gays continue to defend their promiscuous life styles and even their bathhouses. Dr. Franklin Kameny, founding member of the National Gay Task Force, actually argues, "We have no indication that the bathhouses are sources of infection. If the bathhouses were shut down, the influence on the spread of AIDs would be miniscule. Most homosexuals would have more than one partner, whether the bathhouses existed or not." *(Washington Times,* July 21, 1983, p. 2C)

The most telling cover-up, however, appeared in the July, 1983 issue of *California* magazine in an article by Peter Collier and David Horowitz entitled, "White Wash." According to Collier and Horowitz there was a deliberate cover-up by San Francisco's gay leaders to suppress vital information concerning San Francisco's Castor area and AIDS. The gay leaders did not want to admit publicly that gay bathhouses were hot houses for AIDS. Instead, since the bathhouses were the symbol of gay liberation itself, the gay leaders sought to suppress studies tying bathhouse promiscuity to AIDS. Collier and Horowitz even acknowledge that "the present epidemic of AIDS among promiscuous urban gay males is occurring because of the unprecedented promiscuity of the last ten to fifteen years.''

The one vital stat that the gay leaders wanted suppressed was that 1 out of every 333 single men in the Castor area of San Francisco had already been diagnosed as having AIDS. The gay leadership worried that if they admitted the plague was spreading sexually ''everything that had been said about their life style would seem true.''

We close this chapter with a few illustrations of the homosexual life-style. Ask yourself if such activity does not raise serious questions about a nation's moral and spiritual values, its level of tolerance and decency, its hedonism and its survivability. Also, see if you do not agree with George Gilder, who said, ''The usual circuit of gay bars, returning service men, forlorn personal advertisements and street cruises afford gratifications so brief and squalid that society should do everything it can to prevent the spread of the disease.''[78]

## Pancake Make-up

Picture in your mind the following situation as reported in *Time* magazine, October 31, 1969: ''An exclusive formal ball will mark Halloween in San Francisco this week. In couturier gowns and elaborately confected masquerades, the couples will whisk around the floor until 2 a.m., while judges award prizes for the best costumes and the participants elect an 'Empress.' By then the swirling belles will sound more and more deep-voiced, and in the early morning hours dark stubble will sprout irrepressibly through their pancake make-up. The celebrators are all homosexuals.''

Next consider the homosexual bathhouses, which, says *Time* (September 8, 1975), are found in almost all large cities: ''For $5 or $10 a man is entitled to twelve hours and as much sex as he wants. There are usually small private cubicles as well as a large 'orgy room' used for group sex. A customer can go with a partner, pick up a stranger in the 'orgy room', or simply go to a cubicle, leave the door ajar and see who steps in."

Even when the liberated homosexuals go public and put their best foot forward there is still a great deal to be desired. For example, when 50,000 homosexuals marched up Fifth Avenue in New York City under the banner of their "gay flag" (lavender stripes and 50 sex symbols) the lead man had to stop in front of St. Patrick's Cathedral and perform a series of vulgar gyrations. The lesbians and feminists chanted for power. NAMBLA passed out leaflets praising pedophilia, while men and boys walked arm in arm under a banner reading "Man-Boy Love is Beautiful." The Gay Militant Atheists chanted "Smash the state, smash the Church, death to the Church." Some chanted "Pope John Paul, are you gay?" Others sang "Two, four, sex, eight, how do you know the Pope is straight?" When the parade ended in Central Park many of the participants engaged in public sex acts. The gay ideologs, of course, were protected by the pro-homosexual media which showed viewers mostly pictures of ordinary marching bands and two men hugging affectionately.

## Washington's Finest

One of America's most celebrated homosexuals is Dan Bradley, former head of the U.S. Legal Services Corporation. In fact, Bradley is the most senior federal official in American history to declare publicly his homosexuality.

Bradley's homosexual lifestyle, of course, is of the highest level. He is no gay pimp or prostitute. Therefore, his lifestyle is worthy of study and was revealed for us in an article by Taylor Branch entitled "Closets of Power" in the October 1982 issue of *Harper's* magazine.

According to Branch, Bradley's homosexual activity began when a young blond urchin in blue jeans and a T-shirt walked up to Bradley and said, "I'll let you —— me for five dollars."

Later there was Tom. Tom was one of several hundred men packed together on the sandy white beaches of San Juan, Puerto Rico—"all had their slinky little bathing suits and their effeminate mannerisms," says Bradley.

Bradley took Tom back to his hotel room and after a little pina colada and marijuana slept with him.

His homosexual life began in earnest however, in Atlanta, Georgia, at a place called the Varsity. "He found men at the Varsity and brought them home for one-night stands."

He later hooked up with a group of about ten closeted professionals who saw each other on weekends. "One of them would cook dinner for the rest, and they would go out to one or more 'cruising bars' at the 'witching hour' looking for sex."

According to the article, Bradley finally shouted Eureka when he discovered—the gay baths. Says Branch, "As for sex, he made a heartening discovery. He found the baths. Having read about the gay baths, he finally worked up the courage to visit one in Miami. He walked behind the forbidding walls and saw hundreds of gay men wearing towels. It took Bradley about five minutes to discern that the whole place was expressly designed for promiscuous anonymous sex, which was exactly what he had in mind. He felt secure behind the great walls. 'I must have had sex with ten different guys that first night. I was like a kid in a candy store. Nobody talked about what anybody did for a living.'" [80]

Following a production of the musical *Hair,* he "fell under the spell" of one of its male performers and ar-

ranged a rendezvous with him in Washing
Bradley says this was the first male he went
more than once. It was also the partner that com,
his "gay education." He mastered the difference be
tween "nellies," "twinkies," and "chickens." He mastered the "Hankie Code," discovering that if he cruised
a gay bar with a dark blue handkerchief on the left hip,
he was signalling to the boys that he wanted a particular
type of sex.

In Washington, D.C., Bradley soon learned that the
nation's capital takes good care of its gay population.
He went to different gay bars nearly every night (Equus,
Rascals, Eagle) and bumped into lawyers, lobbyists,
bureaucrats, and aides from Capitol Hill. "Some of
Bradley's contemporaries introduced him to some
younger Adonis types among Capitol Hill aides. Those
being his chosen sexual partners, he pursued brief affairs
with a few of them."

He admits attending a gay party in Virginia that
turned out to be an orgy. He ended up in bed with a
"lawyer from the Department of Justice." Bradley said
he found that many closeted officials were in the habit
of sleeping in the early evening so they could party and
"cruise" late at night.

This is the homosexual lifestyle at its finest. Bradley
was the highest federal official to publicly declare his
homosexuality. He touched elbows with homosexual
Congressmen, Capitol Hill aides, lawyers, etc.—the nation's finest practitioners of the homosexual lifestyle.

Is it any wonder why foreign agents hang out amongst
the gay community since much gay gossip consists of
"who's who in the closet?"

Is it any wonder why the "straight" society finds one-
night stands and brief relationships inimical to the family? We have already seen that the high rate of V.D.

spread by the gay community is actually a medical threat to the nation.

If this type of activity, along with the seduction of the youth, homosexual sex crimes, etc. can be condoned by the Christian community and by the general public, America will sink into the dust bin of history.

No nation that allows its young to be enticed into such abominable behavior can survive. For one thing, God will not allow that nation to survive. He destroyed cities and nations in the past for such behavior! "If God doesn't judge America," one said, "he'll owe Sodom and Gomorrah an apology."

1. Enrique T. Rueda, *The Homosexual Network,* p. 37

2. *Newsweek,* April 18, 1983, p. 76.

3. *Ibid.,* p. 80.

4. Bruce Rodgers, *The Queen's Vernacular: A Gay Lexicon* (San Francisco: Straight Arrow Book, 1972).

5. *Time,* March 24, 1980, p. 75.

6. *Ibid.*

7. Peter Fisher, *The Gay Mystique* (New York: Stein and Day, 1975), p. 89.

8. *Time,* October 31, 1969, p. 61-64. Other authorities, e.g., C.A. Allen, *Textbook of Psychosexual Disorders* (1969), lists twelve types of homosexuals.

9. *Eros Defiled,* p. 119.

10. See Zygmund Dobbs, *Keynes at Harvard* (West Sayville, New York: Probe Research, Inc., 1969).

11. C.A. Tripp, *The Homosexual Matrix,* A Signet Book (New York: The American Library, 1975), p. 218.

12. *Newsweek,* February 11, 1980, p. 92C.

13. Frank M. duMas, *Gay Is Not Good,* p. 99.

14. John W. Drakeford, *A Christian View of Homosexuality,* p. 44.

15. John Boswell, *Christianity, Social Tolerance, and Homosexuality* (Chicago: The University of Chicago Press, 1980), p. 370, 1.

16. *The Gay Mystique,* p. 169.

17. *Ibid.,* p. 170.

18. *Christopher Street,* March 1978, p. 54.

19. *Ibid.*

20. See Appendix 8.

21. *National Review,* October 28, 1977, p. 1221.

22. *Time,* January 17, 1983, p. 47.

23. *The London Daily Telegraph,* March 14, 1981, p. 3.

24. Tom O'CArroll, *Paedophilia: The Radical Case* (Boston: Alyson Publications, 1982), p. 9.

25. *Ibid.,* p. 10.

26. *Ibid.,* p. 9.

27. *Ibid.,* p. 18.

28. *Ibid.*

29. *The Guardian,* March 18, 1981, p. 1.

30. Enrique T. Rueda, *The Homosexual Network,* p. 203. The first state to actually reduce the age of sexual consent to 13 years of age was New Jersey. In fact, their law makes sex between even younger children legal if there is less than four years difference in their ages. Those responsible for the new law were two local feminist groups *(Newsweek,* May 7, 1979, p. 36). In a debate I had with Mr. Bob Kuntz of Miami, Florida in April, 1978, Mr. Kuntz admitted the goal of the homosexual community was to reduce the age of sexual consent to 13 years of age.

31. *Chicago Sun-Times,* January 18, 1983.

32. Enrique T. Rueda, *The Homosexual Network,* p. 81

33. *Chicago Sun-Times,* January 18, 1983.

34. *Time,* January 17, 1983, p. 47.

35. *Ibid.*

36. *Ibid.*

37. Rueda, *The Homosexual Network,* p. 177.

38. *Colorado Springs Gazette Telegraph,* January 14, 1983, p. E9.

39. *Tulsa World,* January 6, 1983.

40. *Colorado Springs Gazette Telegraph,* January 14, 1983, p. E9.

41. *Chicago Sun-Times,* January 18, 1983.

42. Rueda, *The Homosexual Network,* p. 202.

43. *Ibid.,* p. 203.

44. *Ibid.,* p. 185.

45. *Ibid.*

46. *Ibid.,* p. 176.

47. *Ibid.,* p. 453.

48. *Time,* September 7, 1981, p. 69.

49. *Ibid.*

50. *Ibid.*

51. *Colorado Springs Gazette Telegraph,* January 14, 1983, p. E9.

52. *Time,* September 7, 1981, p. 69.

53. *National Review,* October 28, 1977, p. 1221.

54. Frank M. duMas, *Gay Is Not Good,* p. 41.

55. *Ibid.,* p. 92.
56. See Appendix 2.
57. See Appendix 3.
58. *The Anita Bryant Story,* p. 136.
59. Dr. Paul Cameron, Committee to Oppose Special Rights for Homosexuals, Box 30605, Lincoln, Nebraska.
60. *Time,* March 28, 1983, p. 53.
61. *Ibid.*
62. *Colorado Springs Sun,* March 24, 1983, p. 10.
63. *Newsweek,* December 21, 1981, p. 51.
64. *Ibid.,* April 18, 1983, p. 75.
65. *Ibid.,* p. 76.
66. *Ibid.,* p. 80.
67. *Ibid.*
68. *MS Magazine,* May 1983, p. 103.
69. *Ibid.*
70. *Newsweek,* December 21, 1981, p. 51.
71. *Colorado Springs Gazette Telegraph,* August 27, 1983, p. A10.
72. Frank M. duMas, *Gay Is Not Good,* p. 29, 111.
73. *Ibid.,* p. 162.
74. *Colorado Springs Gazette Telegraph,* February 1, 1983, p. B6.
75. *Newsweek,* April 18, 1983, p. 80.
76. *Ibid.*
77. *People,* February 14, 1983, p. 43.
78. Rueda, *The Homosexual Network,* p. 49.
79. *Sexual Suicide,* p. 238.
80. *Harper's,* October, 1982, p. 39.

Seattle, Washington, June 25, 1977. Two unidentified young men joined a crowd of 2,000 persons for a march in support of the gay rights movement. The march kicked off Gay Pride Week, a celebration announced by Mayor Wes Uhlman in honor of the contributions homosexuals have made to the city. Courtesy of Wide World Photos. (KM 71600 str/Roy Goodall)

Hollywood, California, December 26, 1969. Pastor Troy Perry, founder of the Sodomy Church, later changed to the Metropolitan Community Church, prefers long-term "monogamous relationships" but confesses his own love life has not been that exclusive. "I believe there can be loving experience, even in a one-night stand." Courtesy of Wide World Photos. (hh60200tms)

Washington, D.C., March 26, 1977. Jean O'Leary and Bruce Voeller, right, co-directors of the National Gay Task Force, hold a press conference following their meeting with Presidential Assistant Midge Constanza at the White House. In the background Rev. Troy Perry. They emerged from the three-hour meeting declaring that it demonstrated that the President's commitment to Human Rights extends to Gay people.
Courtesy of Wide World Photos.

San Francisco, California, June 27, 1982. Police estimated 300,000 gay and gay sympathizers came to celebrate the annual Lesbian/Gay Freedom Day parade down Market Street and the rally in Civic Center Plaza. Courtesy of Wide World Photos (cv11530str-carl viti).

Boston, Mass., June 20, 1981. Under a mass of balloons, proponents of homosexual rights march down Beacon Street during the 11th annual Gay and Lesbian Pride Day. The crowd was estimated to be 10,000 to 12,000. Courtesy of Wide World Photos (jam 71610stf/mcdonnell).

Sacramento, California, June 21, 1977. Supporters of gay rights hold a rally outside the Capitol in Sacramento. They were there to protest a resolution before the Senate Rules Committee by Sen. John Briggs that would have commended Anita Bryant in her fight against homosexuals. The Amendment died in committee. Courtesy of Wide World Photos (WJZ 31400 WJZ)

Miami, Florida, June 28, 1981. 2,500 gay supporters from all over Florida march in the 1981 Gay Pride Day Parade. Not only did Ms. Karen Hanes push son, Courtney, to emphasize her point, but gay motorcycle clubs also were featured in the parade. Courtesy of Wide World Photos (PW11700stf/wright).

New York, December 29, 1982. Spokesman David Thorstead (center) of North American Man Boy Love Association (NAMBLA) at a press conference holding forth a "Boyhood Calendar." Courtesy of Wide World Photos (cd 31355stf/gpaul).

High Island, Texas, August 13, 1973. Authorities carry a body recovered from a shallow grave near High Island to a waiting hearse. Four more bodies have been recovered, bringing to 27, the total known victims in the mass homosexual slayings in Texas. Courtesy of Wide World Photos

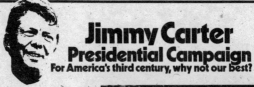

# Jimmy Carter
## Presidential Campaign
### For America's third century, why not our best?

### Rev. Troy Perry:

*"I am strongly supporting Jimmy Carter because of his commitment to civil rights for all people and because of his opposition to non-job related employment discrimination."*

*Rosalynn Carter, Jimmy's wife, discussing community issues with Dr. Newton Deiter (left) and Rev. Troy Perry (center).*

## THE UNANIMOUS CHOICE OF OUR COMMUNITY

| | | | |
|---|---|---|---|
| Sharon D. Cornelison | Jim Kepner | Rev. Troy D. Perry | Clayton Wells |
| Newton Deiter | Morris Kight | Larry Reh | Stuart A. Zinn |
| Howard Fox | Larry Littlejohn | Pat Rocco | |
| David Glascock | Michael Manning | David Schwinkendorf | |
| Albert L. Gordon, Esq. | Terence K. O'Brien, Esq. | Pat Underwood | |

### Jimmy Carter Presidential Campaign

**Southern California Headquarters, 8727 W. Third St. Suite 203, Los Angeles, CA 90048. (213) 273-6250.**

Paid for by the Jimmy Carter Presidential Campaign Committee, R.J. Lipshutz, Treasurer, P.O. Box 1976, Atlanta, GA 30301.

A copy of our report is filed with the Federal Election Commission and is available for purchase from the Federal Election Commission, Washington, D.C.

### Jimmy Carter for President

Yes, I would like to help elect Jimmy Carter our next President. Enclosed is my check for $____.

Name _____ Address _____
City _____ State _____ Zip ____
Place of Employment _____
Occupation _____
Home phone _____ Bus. phone _____

*Please make check payable to: JIMMY CARTER Presidential Campaign, 8727 W. Third St., Suite 203, Los Angeles, CA 90048.*

Los Angeles, California, June 2, 1976. Candidate Jimmy Carter uses the pages of the homosexual newspaper "The Advocate" to publicize a photograph of his wife Rosalynn with homosexual leaders Troy Perry and Newton Deiter. Candidate Carter assured the homosexual community his religious convictions on homosexuality would never interfere with his political stance toward homosexuals.

Chapter 4

# The Politics of Homosexuality

*"Homosexuality, especially when not readily apparent, is an affliction the KGB delights in discovering."*

—*John Barron*

One of the most far-reaching political activities involving homosexuality was former candidate Jimmy Carter's bid for the homosexual vote. And since Jimmy Carter won the 1976 presidential contest by fewer than two million votes, it does not take one very long to realize that the homosexual vote significantly helped put Mr. Carter in the White House.

Carter placed political ads in "The Advocate," one of the leading homosexual publications. The ads showed his wife engaged in conversation with the Rev. Troy Perry, homosexual leader of the Metropolitan Community Church, and with Dr. Newton Deiter, head of Hollywood's "Gay Mafia." Rev. Troy Perry is quoted as saying, "I am strongly supporting Jimmy Carter because of his commitment to civil rights for all people." [1]

Candidate Carter promised he would personally try to remove criminal penalties in federal law against sodomy and related sex acts. His views were carried to the homosexual community via full-page ads in homosexual publications.

Carter's position paper released from his Los Angeles office, dated May 23, 1976, entitled *Jimmy Carter Speaks Out on Gay Rights* reads, "Jimmy Carter has repeatedly expressed his support of gay people, most recently on May 21st at a news conference in San

Francisco. When asked by reporters whether he supported Congresswoman Bella Abzug's amendment to the Civil Rights Act of 1964, the former Georgia Governor said, 'I will certainly sign it, because I don't think it's right to single out homosexuals for special abuse or special harassment.'

"If signed, the amendment would end discrimination against homosexuals in all housing, federally assisted education, public accommodations and hiring, including the military, as well as in other areas.

"Jimmy Carter's record of speaking out on behalf of gay rights has been consistent.

"On March 19th of this year, when appearing on the Tomorrow Show, Carter said, 'I favor the termination of harassment or abuse or discrimination against homosexuals.'

"In a letter to the *Philadelphia Gay News* in March, 1976, Carter wrote, 'I oppose all forms of discrimination against individuals, including discrimination on the basis of sexual orientation. As President, I can assure you that all policies of the Federal Government would reflect this commitment.'

"When Governor Carter was asked how he could reconcile his religious faith with support for gay people's rights, he replied, 'I don't consider myself one iota better than anyone else because I happen to be a Christian, and I have never done anything other than keep strictly separated my political life from my religious life. There would be no conflict in my life as President, having my own personal, deeply felt beliefs.'

"Governor Carter has also gone on record as supporting the National Women's Agenda pro-gay platform."

Candidate Carter's Los Angeles office also circulated a letter by Howard A. Fox, Coordinator of the "Gay Friends of Jimmy Carter." In his May 11, 1976 letter,

Fox wrote, "Jimmy Carter is the choice for President of most respected gay leaders in California.

"The reason for endorsing Governor Carter as our candidate is that he alone, among all the candidates, is making a significant outreach to gay people. Only Jimmy Carter has pledged to issue an executive order banning discrimination based upon sexual orientation in the federal service. Only Jimmy Carter has made specific plans to visit with our community during his California campaign."

It is apparent that Mr. Carter did not forget his debt to the homosexual community. Just two months after his inauguration he invited the homosexual National Gay Task Force to the White House to consult with one of his top aides, Ms. Margaret Constanza.

The press did not fail to report the meeting: "American homosexual leaders emerged from an unprecedented meeting at the White House, declaring talks with a Carter Administration official demonstrated the President's commitment to human rights extended to gay people. The participants (ten members of the National Gay Task Force) said they were assured that Carter was aware of the meeting, and they noted that during his presidential campaign he promised to support legislation aimed at eliminating hiring discrimination within the government on the basis of sexual preference." [2]

It was a three-hour White House session allowing the homosexuals to air their grievances, especially those relating to the present policies of the Immigration and Naturalization Board (which keeps homosexuals from entering the country) and to the Defense Department's policy of discharging homosexuals from the armed services.

Upon leaving the White House, one of the guests was quoted as saying, "Ms. Constanza has given us the power of her office as a door opener." Jean O'Leary of

111

the National Gay Task Force told reporters, "This is the first time in the history of this country that a president has seen fit to acknowledge the rights and needs of some twenty million Americans." [3]

Shortly after the White House gathering with the homosexuals, Ms. Constanza was sent off to Miami to fight Anita Bryant. [4] And while she was fighting Anita Bryant, HUD's Priscilla Banks was back in Washington redefining "the family" to legitimize homosexual marriages and make possible federal housing money for homosexual couples living together.

## Gay's Golden Age

During his presidency, Jimmy Carter allowed homosexuals unlimited access to the White House, allowed homosexuals to place a wreath at the tomb of the unknown soldier, prohibited government agencies from inquiring about the deviant sexual habits of prospective employees, supported legislation to overturn the current ban on homosexual immigrants, supported homosexual teachers in federally-operated classrooms, allowed federal prisons to admit homosexual materials for inmates, allowed ministers of the homosexual denomination (UFMCC) access to federal prisons, allowed UFMCC ministers at the President's Conference on Handicapped Individuals, approved the appointment of Virginia Apuzzo, a homosexual political activist, to the 1980 Democratic Platform Committee, appointed Co-Executive Director of the National Gay Task Force, Jean O'Leary, to the National Commission for the Observance of the International Women's Year, appointed two female homosexuals to the President's Advisory Committee on Women, supported Alan Cranston's bill to allow homosexuals to enter the United States, insisted that the IRS grant 501 (c) 3 tax-exempt status to homosexual organizations, forced the Federal Communications Commission, the U.S. Navy, the Bureau of Prisons, the Job Corps, the Public Health Service, and the Agency for International Development to make pro-homosexual decisions, placed his own mother Lillian at a gay fund raising dinner in Los Angeles, and finally, for the first time in history, adopted and placed a gay-rights plank in the 1980 Democratic Party platform.

No wonder the Carter Presidency has been referred to as the "golden age" of the homosexual movement. No wonder the National Gay Task Force wrote President Carter on January 16, 1981 and expressed its appreciation for "the positive steps taken by your administration to advance the civil rights and human dignity of all gay people." [5] As Rueda points out, it seems the full weight of the federal government was "poised to enact even the most controversial items of the homosexual agenda for America." [6] The political debt had to be paid in full.

Whoever commented, therefore, that the homosexual revolution was being waged at the White House and on Capitol Hill was not being overly dramatic. The gay plague settling over America has been to a great extent the result of pro-homosexual actions taken in Washington, D.C. It will be interesting to see if the same individuals take responsibility for the gay plague's epidemic diseases about to settle over America! The homosexuals "thank you" for being given their human and civil rights has been to pollute our blood banks and cause an epidemic of deadly diseases (traced to their own promiscuous sexual behavior) to cast their black shroud over America.

### Gay Vote Sought

With President Carter breaking the ice on the homosexual issue and with the 1980 Democratic Party Platform's adoption of a gay rights plank, it was only to be expected that the 1984 Democratic Presidential candidates would make a determined bid for the homosexual vote. Or as one writer for the *Los Angeles Times* put it, "A decade ago, a national politician siding with the gay rights lobby, or what there was of one back then, would have been risking political suicide. Today it can be a political death wish not to be for gay rights."[7]

On September 29, 1982, Presidential candidate Walter Mondale was the keynote speaker at a homosexual rights dinner at the Waldorf Astoria Hotel in New York City. The purpose of the dinner was to raise "a campaign war chest to keep our enemies out of the United States Congress and to elect our allies." Tickets for the dinner sold for $150 each and the homosexuals planned to raise $150,000 for advancing their cause of lesbian and gay rights.

"Former Vice President Walter F. Mondale," said Ronald Smothers of the *New York Times*, "appealed to more than 1,000 homosexual rights activists and their supporters last night to join the Democratic Party in fighting what he called the 'irrational discrimination' of the Reagan Administration."[8]

"Of all the principles the Reagan Administration is weakening," said Mondale, "the most important in the long run may well be this country's commitment to universal human rights."

The Presidential candidate drew applause from the homosexual audience when he recalled the 1980 Democratic National Convention's platform contained a plank opposing discrimination based on "sexual orientation." He also drew applause when he cited his party's midterm convention (1982) commitment to "eliminate all laws, rules and regulations which discriminate against individuals on the basis of sexual orientation."[9]

The dinner was termed "a historic moment for the homosexual rights movement." In the past the homosexuals had to go to the politicians and ask them their position on the issues. Now the politicians are coming to the homosexuals.

In fact, according to the *New York Times,* Mr. Mondale and his political command came to Dan J. Bradley, a homosexual and former head of the Legal Services Corporation, for consultation on his speech. The *Times* also reported, "after dinner, Mr. Mondale will be appearing on the ABC News program 'Nightline' to discuss the issue with a number of leaders of the homosexual rights movement." [10] The Nightline program was cancelled when Mr. Mondale refused to appear.

Others sponsoring the dinner were Senator Alan Cranston (D-Cal.), Senator Ted Kennedy (D-Mass.), Sen. Daniel Moynihan (D-NY), New York Governor Mario Cuomo, Rep. Ted Weiss (D-NY), and the Democratic Mayors of Washington, San Francisco, Minneapolis, Boston and Atlanta.

According to Enrique T. Rueda, Senator Cranston, another 1984 Presidential candidate, is a leading supporter of the homosexual movement. Cranston's autographed portrait hangs behind the desk of the director of the Washington Office of the Universal Fellowship of Metropolitan Community Churches (headquarters of the homosexual churches in America). In fact, Cranston's office was the setting for a conference sponsored by the National Gay Task Force as it drew up its long and short term goals for the whole gay rights movement. And at the third annual dinner of Washington, D.C.'s homosexual Gertrude Stein Democratic Club, Cranston insisted that he was the only 1984 presidential candidate in the race with "a clear-cut and positive record on the issue of gay and lesbian rights." [11] In truth, as Rueda points out, "the leftist homosexual coalition seems to have formed right at the U.S. Congress." [12]

Democratic Senators Cranston, Ted Kennedy and Paul Tsongas have all played key roles in the homosexual revolution on Capitol Hill. Soon to join them in earnest seems to be 1984 presidential candidate Senator Gary Hart (D-Colorado).

On April 23, 1983 Senator Hart was the keynote speaker before the sixth anniversary dinner of the Municipal Elections Committee of Los Angeles (MECLA) at the Hollywood Palladium. The group identifies itself as the "oldest and strongest political action committee in the country focusing on gay and feminist issues." [13]

A MECLA fact sheet says its annual dinners are important because of the presence of officeholders and because the "evening is an acknowledgment of these officeholders for supporting gay rights." [14] The spring issue of MECLA's newsletter hails Hart for having made a "strong outreach to the gay and lesbian community" and says his "enthusiastic response to MECLA's invitation is a further indication of his support for our issues." [15] Hart's support of the Democratic Party platform calling for elimination of discrimination based on sexual orientation endears him to the homosexual community, in spite of the fact that such a position would immediately place homosexuals in the military, CIA, FBI and other highly sensitive areas of government. "The conclusion," says Rueda, "that the homosexual movement is a subset of the spectrum of the American liberal movement is inescapable." [16]

## Democrats and Gays

To cement further the relationship between the homosexual movement and the Democratic Party the homosexuals established the National Association of Gay and Lesbian Democratic Clubs in June of 1982. The chairman of the group, Mr. Tom Chorlton, president of the Washington, D.C. Gertrude Stein Democratic Club, and fourteen other members of the National Association of Gay and Lesbian Democratic Clubs met in June with the 1982 Democratic National Party Conference in Philadelphia and decided on how the homosexuals could best help the election of Democrats to Congress.

Chorlton said most politically active homosexuals in the United States "tend to be Democrats because of the party's traditional role as an advocate of the rights of minority groups." [17]

Senator Alan Cranston addressed the new group and said homosexuals were victims of "false stereotypes" and predicted an end to discrimination. "Victory won't come easy, but come it will, I am convinced." [18]

On August 30, 1982 the Chairman of the Democratic National Committee, Charles T. Manatt, wrote Tom Chorlton of the National Association of Gay and Lesbian Democratic Clubs and reiterated their common goals to be "full human rights and civil rights for every American . . . (and) to end any discrimination based on sexual orientation."

On February 4, 1983 in a meeting in Washington, D.C., the Democratic National Committee officially established a "Lesbian and Gay Caucus" within the DNC itself. Such a move significantly increased the power and influence of homosexuals within the Democratic Party. Larry Bush, editor of the homosexual newspaper, *Advocate,* reported in the *Washington Post* that what amazed Ann Lewis, DNC Political director "was that there were no 'fireworks' among Democrats." [19] Bush notes that there was little attention paid to the development "from any quarter" and reasons, "it seems to have been simply the latest installment in the increasingly familiar story of growing gay political influence and acceptance." [20]

According to Tom Chorlton it was the DNC's Chairman Charles Manatt who urged the gays to form the gay caucus. [21] And Peter Vogel admitted that "through this process we have again demonstrated that the gay political movement is indeed nationwide."[22] He also said that the caucus "clearly establishes gay rights as part of the mainstream of the Democratic party's historic commitment to social justice for all Americans."[23]

*Human Events* noted that the increasing gay influence has been dramatic in just the last few years. In 1980 the Democratic party platform included a statement opposing discrimination based on "sexual preference." But in 1982 at the Democratic party mid-term convention, delegates endorsed a legislative approach to the issue calling for expansion of the 1964 Civil Rights Act to prohibit employment discrimination against homosexuals.

"A federal gay civil rights bill in the House backed mostly by liberal Democrats," says *Human Events,* "actually goes beyond the 1982 language and would prohibit discrimination against homosexuals in the areas of housing, public accommodations, federal programs and employment. Conservatives have voiced fears that such an approach would lead to use of affirmative action or quotas to guarantee the 'rights' of homosexuals."[24]

The conclusion says *Human Events* is that this continued pandering to a movement regarded by most Americans as immoral and perverted will certainly "stigmatize the 1984 Democratic party nominee for President."[25]

No homosexual, of course, could wish for more. It gives immediate respectability to the liberated homosexual lifestyle of gay bars, gay bathhouses, gay bookstores, homosexual pornography, homosexual literature and art, homosexual slave auctions, homosexual newspapers, adult homosexual male lovers, adult lesbian female lovers, man/boy lovers, homosexual prostitution, homosexual seduction, homosexual churches (where David and Jonathan are portrayed as homosexual lovers as well as Ruth and Naomi, Jesus and John), homosexual marriages and families, homosexual adoptions, homosexual parades, homosexual discos and balls, homosexual political clubs, homosexual professional clubs, homosexual language, homosexual symbols, homosexual rights platforms, homosexual sadomasochism (S&M), transvestites (drag queens), homosexual leather, homosexual VD clinics and finally, but certainly not least—the Gay Plague (AIDS).

Yet, the very ingredients of the spectrum that make the homosexual movement a homosexual revolution are the very things that Senator Alan Cranston calls "false stereotypes." Would Senator Cranston please portray the whole homosexual lifestyle as he understands it!

If homosexuals are to experience full human rights and civil rights they will be allowed to marry legally and adopt children. They will be placed in the military and in national security positions.

And if there is no discrimination based on sexual orientation then Washington, D.C.'s Acts 4-69 will be implemented which would legalize incest, pederasty, and bestiality.

Before placing homosexuals in sensitive positions, however, it might be well to understand what this fully entails.

## Security Risks

In spite of the pro-homosexual attitude of the Carter administration, certain programs were never fully implemented for reasons stated by *Time* as early as 1975: "Security clearances, either by Government or industry, are still not given to gays because of fear of blackmail." [26]

Also of concern is the fact that homosexuals "personality disorders" can be successfully exploited by foreign agents. Says John Barron, "Contrary to popular supposition, the KGB is not primarily interested in homosexuals because of their presumed susceptibility to blackmail. In its judgment, homosexuality often is accompanied by personality disorders that make the victim potentially unstable and vulnerable to adroit manipulation. It hurts the particular homosexual who, while more or less a functioning member of his society, is nevertheless subconsciously at war with it and himself. Compulsively driven into tortured relations that never gratify, he cannot escape awareness that he is different.''

Barron continues, ''Being different, he easily rationalizes that he is not morally bound by the mores, values and allegiances that unite others in community or society. Moreover, he nurtures a dormant impulse to strike back at the society which he feels has conspired to make him a secret leper. To such a man treason offers the weapons of retaliation.'' [27]

In fact, homosexuals in government have long been recognized as a danger to Western security. Countess R.G. Waldeck, a Ph.D from the University of Heidelberg, described the ''Homosexual International'' as constituting ''a worldwide conspiracy that has spread all over the globe; has penetrated all classes; operates in armies and in prisons; has infiltrated the press, the movies and the cabinets; and it all but dominates the arts, literature, theater, music and TV.'' [28]

She went on to point out the reason that homosexual officials are a peril to us in the present struggle between West and East: ''Members of one conspiracy are prone to join another conspiracy. This is one reason why so many homosexuals, already enemies of society in general, become enemies of Capitalism in particular. Without being necessarily Marxist, they serve the end of the Communist International *in the name of their rebellion against the prejudices, standards, and ideals of the 'bourgeois' world.''*

She concluded, "The Homosexual International has become a sort of auxiliary of the Communist International. This is the more alarming since the homosexuals are multiplying as the sand upon the seashore."

Although well-financed homosexual organizations are trying to change U.S. national security regulations, it is nevertheless recognized that homosexuals are risks and are thus barred from holding sensitive positions in government.

The armed forces, for example, reportedly dismiss a yearly average of 2,000 men and women for homosexuality. A January, 1981 Department of Defense Fact Sheet bluntly states that it is official policy "that homosexuality is incompatible with military service," and that separation for homosexuals from the military is "mandatory." The statement says, "The presence of such members adversely affects the ability of the Armed Forces to maintain discipline, good order, and morale; to foster mutual trust and confidence among service members; to insure the integrity of the system of rank and command; to facilitate assignment and worldwide deployment of service members who frequently must live and work under close conditions affording minimal privacy; to recruit and retain members of the Armed Forces; to maintain the public acceptability of military service; and to prevent breaches of security." [29]

Until the Carter Administration, the Immigration and Naturalization Service would not grant alien resident status to homosexuals. The State Department is forbidden to employ them, as prescribed by Executive Order 10450. These statutes have not, however, prevented deviates from obtaining government jobs—some of which involve sensitive national security positions.

In August, 1960, two employees of the National Security Agency (NSA) fled to Russia and gave highly important information to the Soviets. The defectors, William

Martin and Bernon Mitchell, were homosexuals who had been permitted access to classified information.

In January, 1981, *Time* magazine revealed that an unidentified mid-level National Security Agency employee had successfully challenged his being fired as a homosexual. According to *Time,* "He won the right to keep his job as a technical analyst despite his homosexuality, but only after agreeing to lessen the danger of blackmail by disclosing his sexual preference to his family." [30]

Intelligence experts, however, do not believe that this will alleviate the problem. Says Cord Meyer, former assistant deputy director for operations, "The Soviets specialize in homosexual cases. They assign KGB agents who are homosexuals themselves to entrap our agents." [31]

Another CIA official said, "Homosexual agents tend to flock together. Once you get a homosexual cell, they take care of each other." [32] His prime example was the case of Kim Philby in England, who led a small group of homosexuals, educated at Cambridge, who sold British secrets to the Soviets during and after World War II.

Since homosexuals betray their country for any number of reasons (blackmail, believes Marxism is pro-homosexual, getting even for being ostracized as a homosexual, enjoys dual roles, teaching their country a lesson for rejecting their homosexual lifestyle, etc.) homosexuals in sensitive government positions are dangerous and the situation must be remedied. However, even now the homosexuals have a new campaign under way to repeal the State Department's executive order banning homosexual employment and National Gay Task Force Washington director Jeff Levi said, "I think it's long overdue that Executive Order 10450 be removed from the books." [33] Representatives of the Gay Task Force are claiming that "there has been no evidence of foreign agents obtaining national security information by threatening to expose an employee's homosexuality." [34]

CIA spokesperson Katryn Riedel countered the homosexual claim by stating, "foreign intelligence services are known to target for cultivation and exploitation persons known or believed to be practicing adult homosexual behavior. There have been a significant number of espionage cases in which homosexual conduct has been a factor. In addition, homosexual activity is illegal in many areas of the world in which agency personnel must serve." [35]

To reinforce the notions that the KGB would have a field day recruiting our homosexuals in security positions, Frank McNamara observed that "the great majority of gay groups that have been politically active in recent years have espoused the most radical anti-U.S. causes." [36] In other words, the gay liberationists are already at war with America.

The State Department, in one instance in 1963, discovered a colony of thirty-two homosexuals who were forced to resign. More recently, U.S. Ambassador to Argentina Robert C. Hill testified that, when he was Assistant Secretary of State, 14,000 homosexuals had been removed from the State Department.

The cases noted above hardly have scratched the surface. It is not known how many homosexuals are now holding government jobs. The most recent report we could locate dates back to 1964, when the President of the homosexual Mattachine Society, Dr. Franklin Kameny, testified that "there are about 200,000 to a quarter of a million homosexuals in the government."

It should be noted that the founder of the Mattachine Society, Henry Hay, was himself an admitted Communist and an avowed homosexual. Hay organized the Society in the late 1940's as a "service and welfare organization devoted to the protection and improvement of society's androgynous minority." Hay also was concerned with what he considered militant American Fascism against gays.

In bygone days the Mattachine Society was referred to as "Bachelors Anonymous" and "International Bachelors Fraternal Order for Peace and Social Dignity." It was originally conceived as an underground operation, including secret membership.

Hay, himself, was a member of the Communist Party for eighteen years, until he became so involved in his homosexual movement that he requested expulsion from the Communist Party for the good of the Party. The Party finally dropped him from its membership, noting Hay to be a "lifelong friend of the people."

Now in the 1980's we have a reincarnation of Henry Hay in the person of NAMBLA's David Thorstad. Thorstad not only believes homosexuality is good for everyone, children included, but he also sees himself "as a revolutionary Marxist and a Leninist." [37] According to Thorstad, "Christianity and Capitalism have destroyed the ability of most people to even recognize in themselves the ability to love someone of the same sex." [38] To show that he means business, Thorstad sent out his 1978 Christmas cards inscribed, "Revolutionary, Homosexual, Atheist." [39]

Thorstad, of course, is simply practicing good Marxist/Leninism. Lenin made it clear that before a Communist revolution can be undertaken the moral standards of the targeted nation must be undermined. Garth Lean, in his work *Brave Men Choose,* quotes Lenin: "Postpone operations until the moral disintegration of the enemy makes delivery of the mortal blow inevitable and easy." [40]

Lean also notes that a bishop's son who had become a Communist agent in Scandanavia told him that his instructions were not to mention Marxism to the youth for some years. Instead, says Lean, the agent was told "to encourage heterosexual and homosexual looseness," and "when they can no longer say 'No' to themselves, they will be unable to say 'No' to Communism." [41] Now we know why Soviet Ambassador to Sweden, Mm. Kollontai, reported to Lenin, "Immorality in the schools is progressing satisfactorily." [42]

## KGB and Gays

Soviet intelligence agencies long have tried to take advantage of the presence of homosexuals in Western governments. The KGB's Second Chief Directorate employs 25,000 officers, agents and civilian informants whose job it is, working through the Tourism Department, to subvert visiting foreigners. Quite often the Secret Police are then able to keep tabs on a prospective informant when he returns to the U.S. by means of the vast KGB network that flourishes in this country today.

Former Naval Intelligence Operative George Hiscott points out that "40 percent of the Soviet officials under diplomatic status are in fact KGB professionals." He estimates there are probably 1900 KGB agents on station in the U.S. including "illegals" and "sleepers". These agents then develop their own network of subagents and contacts, recruited from the native population.

John Barron, in his definitive study, *KGB,* reports that "homosexuality, especially when not readily apparent, is an affliction the KGB delights in discovering."

Bob Reguly, writing in the *Toronto Sun,* likewise admitted, "The prevalence of homosexuals in government enabled the Soviet Union's KGB spy network to score its greatest post-war successes in Ottawa." [43] Reguly relates how Canadian Prime Minister Trudeau sought to stem the drain of senior civil service talent by easing up on security restrictions for homosexuals. Since so many top members of the external affairs department were being investigated "and seen at orgies" the Prime Minister opted for keeping them in the department if they accepted medical treatment.

Nevertheless, says Reguly, "the Russians never eased up one bit in blackmailing homosexuals in government. Many had families to conceal it from. It's still a Sodom and Gomorrah in Ottawa." [44]

The success of the KGB in recruiting homosexuals could not be better illustrated than what has happened to England (and indirectly to America since some of England's traitors served in Washington, D.C.) in the persons of Maclean, Burgess, Philby, Blunt and Driberg. The sordid story of Soviet agents and homosexuality is described in detail in Andrew Boyle's *The Fourth Man* and Chapman Pincher's *Their Trade is Treachery.*

Anthony Blunt, says Chapman Pincher, "was one of the most damaging spies ever to operate in Britain." [45] He prejudiced many American operations and endangered their personnel "because he informed the Russians about the American Intelligence organization, the Office of Strategic Services." [46] Blunt was a Cambridge don in the 1930's where he recruited his homosexual friends and lovers as Soviet agents. According to Pincher, Blunt was attracted to the Communist Guy Burgess. "Both were homosexuals" says Pincher, "and fellow members of the exclusive group known as the Apostles, whose major topic of conversation was Communism and its merits." [47]

Philby joined the Communist Party in the early 30's and by 1934 was recruited by Soviet intelligence. He was a double agent and was responsible for the escape of Burgess and Maclean to Moscow. The unspeakable damage he and his two homosexual friends did to the West will probably never be known. Philby alone actively betrayed hundreds of British intelligence agents to their death. When he himself fled to Moscow he was put to work in the foreign department of the State Publishing House.

Philby's homosexuality was triggered at boys school. According to David Lewis, "As in many single-sex boarding schools, homosexuality was rife at Westminster, and Philby indulged in it with the other boys. Later he talked openly of having 'buggered and been buggered' at school." [48]

Tom Driberg was actually the chairman of the Labour Party, a British security agent (MI5), and a KGB agent. He was also a compulsive homosexual, "repeatedly caught either procuring or commiting a homosexual act in public places." [49] In *Their Trade is Treachery* Pincher reports, "Driberg's long relationship with MI5 solves the mystery of why such a notorious homosexual, who was repeatedly caught in the act publicly by the police, was never successfully prosecuted." [50] Boyle notes in his book *The Fourth Man* that it was Driberg who introduced Burgess to the "large underground urinal" in the center of Moscow which was "open all night and frequented by hundreds of questing Slav homosexuals." [51]

Donald Maclean not only gave away British diplomatic codes and cyphers, but betrayed American nuclear secrets. Maclean, says Pincher, "had a pass to the Atomic Energy Commission headquarters that allowed him access without an escort, a privilege denied even J. Edgar Hoover." [52] According to Boyle it was Guy Burgess who introduced Maclean "to the sad pleasures of sodomy." [53]

Burgess was militantly gay, or as Sutherland puts it, "entirely homosexual," and "made not the slightest attempt to conceal it. Rather he flaunted it pursuing men with all the unabashed enthusiasm of a Piccadilly prostitute." [54] Boyle notes that even through the blackout of war-time London Burgess was constantly in search of "delectable youth," [55] and during what Churchill once described as the twilight war (nine months of little action) Burgess indulged his appetite "to the full." [56] According to Sutherland, Burgess, like Oscar Wilde "preferred boys from the working class," whom he would lend to his friends, "including Anthony Blunt." [57] When in Washington, D.C. he was constantly fraternising with the gay community. Boyle reports that Burgess was bound to his Cambridge contacts "intellectually, emotionally and sometimes physically as an active member of what has since been aptly nicknamed the 'Homintern (Homosexual International).'" [58]

Blunt was instrumental in recruiting the American Michael Straight into the Soviet espionage circle when he was a student at Cambridge. Straight was sent back to the States to become a high-level mole. He performed admirably.

American politicians seeking to place homosexuals in positions of national security under the guise of fighting "job discrimination" are asking for a repeat of England's problems with "atheists, Marxists, and sodomites."

## Homintern

*Time* magazine spoke of a homosexual "homintern" and asked the question, "Is there a homosexual conspiracy afoot to dominate the arts and other fields?" [59]

*Time* answers, "Sometimes it seems that way." A gay boss uses his influence to help gay friends. And before long the circle is closed and the gays dominate. The music world, the theater, the art world, painting, dance, fashion, hair dressing, interior design are all heavily saturated and dominated by the "homintern."

## Appeasement

The direct danger of such activity has been set forcefully before the American people in an article in *Harper's* magazine entitled, "The Culture of Appeasement." by the editor of *Commentary,* Norman Podhoretz. [60]

Mr. Podhoretz parallels the cultural matrix of England following World War I with the United States following the Vietnam conflict. He observes the vast similarities between England's reaction to the military build-up of Hitler and our present reaction to the Communist military build-up. For example, while Hitler rearmed, England responded in four distinct stages. First, it was claimed that reports of German rearmament were grossly exaggerated; second, it finally was admitted that the reports were true, but since Germany was so far behind, she never could catch up; third, it further was admitted that Germany had parity with England, but that this was no threat since the Germans had enemies in the East to worry about; fourth, when the full extent of German superiority was acknowledged, it was said that now survival was the main issue and the counsels of appeasement prevailed.

Podhoretz quotes Richard Pipes, who describes America's response to the present Soviet military build-up. Stated Pipes, "The frenetic pace of the Soviet nuclear build-up was explained first on the ground that the Russians had a lot of catching up to do, then that they had to consider the Chinese threat and finally on the grounds that they are inherently a very insecure people and should be allowed an edge in deterrent capability."

As Podhoretz observes, not only is the free world under siege, but we have reached stage three. Stage four seems right around the corner with our nuclear freeze advocates already counseling appeasement.

But the parallel between England and the United States does not end here. There is another ingredient of major value that led to England's inability to cope with Hitler. England's "bright young things" thought England to be so very puritanical in its morals and drearily middle class in its culture that almost any alternative society would do. Thousands of England's upper class young men were signing the Oxford Pledge never to fight for King or Country, and there was a great movement between World War I and World War II to "completely and finally rebel" against England.

Why? Podhoretz writes, "That Auden and Burgess were homosexuals clearly had something, perhaps everything, to do with their need 'completely and finally to rebel against England.' And indeed, it is impossible to read books like *Children of the Sun* or Paul Fussel's *The Great War and Modern Memory* without being struck by the central role that homosexuality played in the entire rebellious ethos of the interwar period in England. Much of the literature of the first world war itself, says Fussel, who has made a very thorough study of it was 'replete' with homosexual passion."

Podhoretz continues, however, "But if homosexual feeling was aroused by the war, homosexual feeling also accounted for a good deal of the pacifism which rose out of the trenches and into the upper reaches of the culture after the war was over. In war poem after war poem and in memoir after memoir, the emphasis was on youthful, masculine beauty so wantonly wasted by the war, the bodies meant for embrace by their own kind that were consigned so early to the grave."

Podhoretz quotes Capt. Ralph Nicholas Chubb's biographer to the effect that Chubb "watched the slaughter of a boy, a creature such as those he had always mentally, and once physically, loved...The boy, a beloved object, was not only forbidden by law to be loved by an adult male but was legally sacrificed by the same laws in the service of his country."

This climate of homosexuality nearly brought England to her knees. At this time in England's history heterosexuality was considered a middle class bore. At Oxford, according to John Betjeman, generally it was only state-subsidized undergraduates who were heterosexual. The "best people" looked to other men for sex and romance. The Audens, Wildes, Burgess, Wilfred Owens, Lytton Stracheys, John Maynard Keynes and thousand more like them were responsible for the moral and political climate that placed England in such a terrible predicament.

In Michael Holroyd's work, *Lytton Strachey, A Critical Biography,* the world was to learn of the gross sexual debaucheries of England's Fabian Socialist leaders. Homosexuality, sado-masochism, lesbianism and the deliberate policy of corrupting the young was the established practice of this large and influential group which eventually set the political and cultural tone for the British Empire.

John Maynard Keynes' sexual partner, Lytton Strachey, admitted that their sexual attitudes could be infiltrated "subtly, through literature, into the bloodstream of the people." Strachey also admits that Keynes (folk hero to thousands of America's economic "jet set") was a "liberal and a sodomite, an atheist and a statistician," who always was ready to guide others to Tunis resort areas where "bed and boy were also not expensive."

Zygmund Dobbs remarks in his work *Keynes at Harvard,* "In academic deviate circles, Keynes acquired underground fame as a skilled connoisseur who was able to spot potential material for future debauchment among the male children at Eton (eight to sixteen years of age), as well as the youth of Cambridge."[61]

And Strachey concedes that the letters passing between himself and Keynes would have "provoked curiousity in Gomorrah and caused the inhabitants of Sodom to sit up and take note."

The similarities in our nation are obvious. Keynes' academic and sexual disciples are legion. As Podhoretz says, "Anyone familiar with homosexual apologetics in America today will recognize those attitudes...suitably updated and altered to fit contemporary American realities, they are purveyed by such openly homosexual writers as Allen Ginsberg, James Baldwin and Gore Vidal—not to mention a host of less distinguished publicists, in whose work we find the same combination of pacifism (with Vietnam naturally standing in for World War I), hostility to one's own country and its putatively dreary middle class way of life and derision of the idea that it stands for anything worth defending..."

America stands before the Communist enemy much like England stood before the Nazi enemy. To make homosexuality as respectable as England did in the twenties and thirties is to invite disaster. England at least had America for help. We would have no one.

The hour is late. We must publicly and privately stand for spiritual and moral values as revealed by God in the Bible and stand resolutely against the homosexual revolution, or we, too, will die.

1. *The Advocate,* A Special California Political Supplement, June 2, 1976, p. 8.

2. *Associated Press,* March 27, 1977.

3. *Ibid.*

4. *The Anita Bryant Story,* p. 128, 129.

5. Enrique T. Rueda, *The Homosexual Network,* p. 447.

6. *Ibid.,* p. 443.

7. *Los Angeles Times,* October 5, 1982.

8. *New York Times,* September 30, 1982, p. 16B. Although the *New York Times* index lists the Mondale speech before the homosexual group in New York the microfilm edition of the *Times* deleted the story.

9. *Ibid.*

10. *New York Times,* September 28, 1982. p. B10.

11. *Human Events,* May 7, 1983, p. 2.

12. Rueda, *The Homosexual Network,* p. 434.
13. *Los Angeles Times,* April 24, 1983, p. 31.
14. *Washington Times,* April 13, 1983, p. 4A.
15. *Ibid.*
16. Rueda, *op. cit.* p. XIX.
17. *Philadelphia Inquirer,* June 25, 1982.
18. *Ibid.*
19. *Washington Post,* March 13, 1983, p. B4.
20. *Ibid.*
21. *Human Events,* February 19, 1983, p. 4.
22. *Ibid.*
23. *Ibid.*
24. *Ibid.*
25. *Ibid.*
26. *Time,* September 8, 1975, p. 36.
27. *Human Events,* May 14, 1983, p. 5.
28. See Appendix 29.
29. *Human Events,* May 14, 1983, p. 6.
30. *Time,* January 12, 1981, p. 22.
31. *Ibid.*
32. *Ibid.*
33. *Human Events,* May 14, 1983, p. 6.
34. *Ibid.*
35. *Ibid,* p. 5.
36. *Ibid.*
37. *Colorado Springs Gazette Telegraph,* January 14, 1983, p. E9.
38. *Ibid.*
39. *Ibid.*
40. Vincent P. Miceli, *The Gods of Atheism* (New Rochelle, New York: Roman Catholic Books, 1971), p. 112.
41. *Ibid.*
42. *Ibid.*
43. *Toronto Sun,* March 30, 1981.
44. *Ibid.*
45. Chapman Pincher, *Their Trade is Treachery* (New York: Bantam Books, 1982), p. 106.
46. *Ibid.,* p. 114.
47. *Ibid.,* p. 108.
48. David Lewis, *Sexpionage: The Exploitation of Sex by Soviet Intelligence* (New York: Harcourt, Brace, Jovanovich, 1976), p. 113.
49. *London Daily Mail,* March 25, 1981, p. 1.
50. Pincher, *op. cit.,* p. 224.
51. Andrew Boyle, *The Fourth Man* (New York: Bantam Books, 1980), p. 411.

52. Pincher, *op. cit.,* p. 224.

53. Boyle, *op. cit.,* p. 163.

54. Donald Sutherland, *The Great Betrayal* (New York: Times Books, 1980), p. 44.

55. Boyle, *op. cit.,* p. 90.

56. *Ibid.*

57. Sutherland, *op. cit.,* p. 56.

58. Boyle, *op. cit.,* p. 136.

59. *Time,* October 31, 1969, p. 61.

60. *Harper's,* October, 1977, p. 25f.

61. Zygmund Dobbs, *Keynes at Harvard* (West Sayville, New York: Probe Research, Inc., 1969), p. 114f.

Chapter 5

## The Bible and Homosexuality

*"There is the possibility of morally good
homosexual relationships."*

—*John J. McNeill*

One of the most important segments of society advocating and defending the homosexual lifestyle is the religious community.

"Churches, once they have been infiltrated by the homosexual movement," says Enrique T. Rueda, "constitute one of its most important allies."[1] He then devotes 140 pages of his book *The Homosexual Network* to tracing this infiltration, listing names of religious homosexual organizations and their leaders. He traces the infiltration of the homosexual movement in the Protestant, Jewish and Roman Catholic churches.

*Christianity Today* carried an article entitled, "Gays Are Gaining Acceptance in More Churches." The article states that the Minnesota Council of Churches is now urging its members to welcome homosexuals and support gay rights legislation. A statement of the Council says *Christianity Today* "contains unprecedented language in support of homosexuality."[2] The statement implies "that homosexual practice is not sinful" and reads, "There may be creative and whole expressions of one's sexuality at various levels in relationships between men and women, between men and other men, and between women and other women."[3]

In a related development, the court of the United Methodist Church's annual conference ruled unanimously (nine-member court) that nothing in United Methodist church law prohibits the ordination of a homosexual. [4]

This ruling was consistent with a 1974 United Methodist Council on Youth Ministries decision that "homosexual practice should not be a bar to the ministry of that denomination." [5]

By 1977 the Episcopal church ordained a practicing homosexual and the Church of England published a report stating (1) homosexuality is good, and (2) homosexuality is unBiblical and a perversion of our moral nature. Dr. Kenneth S. Kantzer referred to the report as "perfect double-speak." [6]

In 1978 a United Presbyterian task force declared "the orientation of practicing homosexuals is consistent with the standards of the denomination. It approved," says Dr. Kantzer, "the homosexual lifestyle and argued that each local presbytery should decide for itself what it would do in handling the issue." [7]

"In short," says Dr. Kantzer, "every major denomination has spawned its group of homosexual enthusiasts." [8]

The Roman Catholic Church is being accused of being out of step with the times and being asked to rethink its traditional sexual morality and support the gay-rights movement. In a report of its San Francisco Commission on Social Justice the Catholic Church is being asked to welcome gays into the priesthood, upgrade service to the gay community, eliminate sexual-preference screening for parochial school jobs, adoption or foster care, encourage gay students at parochial schools and acknowledge the unique spiritual experience of devout homosexual Catholics. [9] Instead of contending that homosexuality is a sin against nature the Catholic Church is being pressured to agree that homosexuality is an inseparable part of some people's nature. Says *Time* magazine: "Though the liberal wing of the U.S. Catholic Church has repeatedly sought to take the U.S. Catholic hierarchy leftward into the new morality, this is the first time a church panel within any U.S. diocese has gone so far as to accept homosexual behavior." [10]

## Metro Community Churches

The most significant homosexual infiltration into the religious community, however, has been the Universal Fellowship of Metropolitan Community Churches. This homosexual denomination is referred to by Rueda as being "at the center of the network of homosexual religious congregations." [11]

Rueda notes that during the Carter Administration the number of homosexual organizations applying for federal grants "was so large that the UFMCC Washington Office counted among its 'constituent services' tracking the progress of grant applications to Federal agencies."

UFMCC's founder Troy Perry boasts that his homosexual denomination was instrumental in helping see that gay caucuses were formed in the United Methodist Church, the United Presbyterian Church, the Presbyterian Church, USA, the Episcopal Church and the Roman Catholic Church. [12]

Perry's homosexual denomination is presently knocking at the door of the National Council and World Council of Churches, seeking admittance for membership. The liberal leadership of both councils might accept the Perry group in a minute, but the fear is that the more conservative members of the various denominations might get upset and demand the withdrawal of their denominations from such liberal, pro-homosexual councils. Since both the National and World Council of Churches have been taking a beating for their pro-Marxist tendencies the leadership might decide not to add pro-homosexual to the pro-Marxist charge. Indeed, *Time* reported that the NCC will decide the issue in May, 1984, although at this time "the homosexual church has little chance of being accepted." [13] During a NCC session in San Francisco some denominations hinted they'd quit the Council if the homosexual church was accepted. Liberal theologian Roy Sano said the NCC should "fear for its soul" if it spurned the gay church. [14] Other delegates called the acceptance of the homosexual church "unthinkable" and a delegate from the African Methodist Episcopal Church called homosexuality "an aberration and perversion." [15]

Be that as it may, UFMCC spokesman R. Adam DeBaugh admits that his group works closely with both the National Council of Churches and the World Council of Churches as well as the Ecumenism Research Agency, the NCC Commission on Women in Ministry, the NCC Joint Strategy and Action Coalition and the Washington Inter-religious Staff Council. [16]

When 70,000 Christians presented President Carter a petition in opposition to the granting of special legal privileges to homosexuals, the homosexual religious leaders and organizations immediately sprang into action. Twenty-one homosexual religious groups met in the White House (April 28, 1980) to protest the petition and the Washington for Jesus rally.

The core of the homosexuals' religious leadership involved in that significant White House meeting included: Rev. Nancy Wilson, R. Adam DeBaugh and Ken Spaats of UFMCC; Frank Scheuren, Elinor Crocker and Joseph Totten of Dignity; Martin Rock of Brethren/Mennonite Council of Gay Caucuses; Raymond Spitale of Gay People in Christian Science; Dr. Ralph Blair and Dr. Wayne Swift of Evangelicals Concerned; Larry Neff and Barrett Brick of Bet Mishpochel (Gay synagogue in Washington, D.C.); John Laurent of

Affirmation (Gay and Lesbian Mormons); Bob Bouchard of Kinship (Seventh Day Adventists); Bruce Grimes and Geoff Kaiser of Friends Committee for Lesbian and Gay Concerns; Robert P. Wheatley of Unitarian-Universalist Office of Gay Concerns; Gabrial Lance of *Insight* Magazine; Rev. William R. Johnson of Lesbian/Gay Ecumenical Center of New York; Dr. James Tinney; Rev. Robert Nugent, and Sister Jeannine Gramick and Rick Garcias of New Ways Ministry; Barbara MacNair, Rick Mixon and Sandra Rogers of American Baptist Concerned; Rev. Jan Griesinger and Rev. Oliver Power of United Churches of Christ Coalition for Gay Concerns; Rev. Michael Collins, Peggy Harmon, Joan Clark and Rev. Bill Matson of Affirmation (United Methodists for Lesbian and Gay Concerns); Howard Erickson and Rev. John Backe of Lutherans Concerned; Dianne Stevenson and Dennis Buckland of Unitarian-Universalist Gay Concerns; William Silver and Sandy Brawders of Presbyterians for Gay Concerns; and Roger Conant of Integrity. [17]

## Religious Bars

Rueda mentions that following the White House meeting the homosexual group attended a luncheon at a Washington, D.C. "leather bar." He feels that Christians might find it significant that the religious homosexual network met in a "leather bar" whose trademark is "a young musclebound, shirtless youth, wearing tight black pants and sporting a whip poised to strike, his genitals exposed and superimposed on an eagle, one of whose wings is about to enfold him." [18]

Christians might also find it significant to learn that mainline denominations are already working on a national Gay Rights bill (introduced in the U.S. Senate by Sen. Paul Tsongas [D-Mass.]); that ministers were present at the founding of the North American Man/Boy

Love Association (NAMBLA) and voiced their endorsement of love between men and boys; that the Jesuit publication *American* finds application of Scripture texts that condemn homosexuality "dubious at best" and has actually offered a qualified endorsement to the proposition that homosexuals should be ordained to the priesthood. [19]

If that isn't enough there's always Dignity's founder Fr. John McNeill, a pro-gay Jesuit priest, hinting that Jesus and John the Apostle were homosexual lovers. [20] It is Dignity's position that "being gay is a blessing, not a curse." [21]

And nearly as disgusting is United Church of Christ's Rev. William R. Johnson who sees, "women's liberation and gay liberation as movements of the Holy Spirit." [22] It perhaps should be noted that the United Church of Christ has already prepared a study guide in anticipation of ordination of homosexuals to the church's ministry. "It would seem," the guide says, "that a gay or lesbian person would be subject to the same understanding, procedures, and criteria for ordination as would any candidate for the ministry." [23]

The Rev. Cecil Williams defends his homosexuality on the basis that "there are no (moral) absolutes," [24] and the Rev. G. William Sheek, director of the National Council of Churches Family Ministries and Human Sexuality Program, says he is deeply concerned about "certain myths and stereotypes that are being perpetuated in the dialogue over the ordinance concerning civil rights for homosexuals."

The National Council spokesman says that "it is simply not true that the Bible has a single and clear position on homosexuality and that the Biblical position was that homosexuality was a sin against nature not to be tolerated in society." [25]

However, it certainly does not take a theologian to see

that the Biblical norm always has been male and female. Even neo-orthodox Karl Barth stated, "The command of God shows him (the homosexual) irrefutably—in clear contradiction of his own theories—that as a man he can only be genuinely human with a woman, or as women with a man." And neo-orthodox Helmut Thielicke stated, "Homosexuality is in every case not in accord with the order of creation."

Some homosexuals frankly admit that "homosexuality is condemned in both the Old and New Testaments." However, generally these homosexuals do not really care what the Bible says, since it is not of great import to them anyway.

## Male and Female

The Bible states, "God created man in his own image, in the image of God created He him, *male and female created He them.*" (Gen. 1:27)

One of God's first commands to man was that he "leave his father and mother and cleave unto his wife." (Gen. 2:24)

Indeed, we are told that in marriage the male and female "shall be one flesh," and that they are to be "fruitful and multiply." (Gen. 1:28) This command obviously never could be fulfilled in any homosexual relationship.

The New Testament counterpart to Genesis 2:24, Ephesians 5:31, 32, states, "For this cause shall a man leave his father and mother, and shall be joined unto his wife, and they two shall be one flesh. This is a great mystery: but I speak concerning Christ and the church." Obviously the relationship of Christ to His Church is typified by the relationship of husband to wife. Again, such a type is destroyed by homosexuality. Homosexuality is not only contrary to God's creative plan and to nature itself but also is contrary to His divine types.

What God clearly says concerning homosexuality in Scripture gives the lie to Rev. G. William Sheek's point that "Scripture does not have a single and clear position on the subject." Scripture consistently and forthrightly condemns homosexuality as being evil and wicked.

## Men of Sodom

In Gen. 13:13 we are told that "the men of Sodom were wicked and sinners before the Lord exceedingly." In Gen. 18:20 we're told "...the cry of Sodom and Gomorrah is great...because their sin is very grievous."

Man in his sin undoubtedly fell into homosexuality as a mark of defiance against God and of confusion among men. It seems that whatever God condemns, man— some way, somehow—twists and perverts into a desirable object. Man's practice of confusing the sex roles and of confusing the biological and theological purpose behind sex must be recorded as one of his most base accomplishments.

The homosexual community obviously is very touchy about Sodom and Gomorrah. Indeed, the homosexual would have us believe that the sin of Sodom has nothing to do with homosexuality. Some argue that Sodom's sin is adultery and incest. Fr. John O'Neill, in his work *The Church and the Homosexual,* argues very weakly that the sin of Sodom is the sin of being poor hosts. [26] John Boswell in his *Christianity, Social Tolerance and Homosexuality* argues the same point, [27] as do most prohomosexual religious writers. One pro-homosexual writer, however, has pointed out that such an interpretation of Genesis 19 does not hold up under scrutiny. Tom Horner in his *Jonathan Loved David* admits "all such positions, and variations upon them, stem ultimately from a study by Derrick Sherwin Bailey, which contends that the verb 'to know' in Genesis 19:5 does not mean 'to have intercourse with'—the men of Sodom that night only wanted to examine the credentials of two mysterious strangers. Unfortunately his exegesis simply cannot stand up."[28]

It can't stand up because of Genesis 19:5 and 7: "Where are the men which came into thee this night? Bring them out unto us *that we may know them,*" and "brethren, do not so wickedly."

The Hebrew word for "know" is *yadha,* meaning "a sexual knowledge or relationship." The men of Sodom desired a homosexual relationship with Lot's guests. If the sin were merely the sin of being poor hosts, Lot never would have offered his own daughters to these bi-sexual perverts. He would have offered them tea and cookies! Incidentally, the same Hebrew word is used in Gen. 19:8: "Behold now, I have two daughters which have not *known* men." Virtually every Biblical scholar agrees that this word, in both instances refers to sexual intercourse.

One hardly can imagine reading such expressions as "the iniquity of the city" (Gen. 19:15) or as "the cry of them is waxen great before the face of the Lord, and the Lord hath sent us to destroy it" (Gen. 19:13) or Lot's admonition to the men of Sodom, "I pray you, breth-ren, do not so wickedly" (Gen. 19:7) if the Sodomites were merely guilty of the sin of inhospitality.

## Filthy Dreamers

If the Lord took such actions upon Sodom because it was a city of poor hosts and hostesses, there would be few cities around today. The truth is that the Lord rained brimstone and fire down upon Sodom and Go-morrah because the two cities and the cities of the plain about them gave themselves over to the shameful prac-tice of homosexuality, including the vice of pederasty (Gen. 19:4). In the words of Scripture, they were "going after strange flesh." (Jude 1:7) Jude refers to the inhabitants of Sodom as "filthy dreamers" who "defile the flesh." (Jude 1:8)

Peter's commentary on Sodom and Gomorrah stating, "...God spared not the angels that sinned, but cast them down to hell...turned the cities of Sodom and Gomorrah into ashes, condemned them with an overthrow, making them an example unto these that after should live ungodly, and delivered just Lot, vexed with the filthy manner of living of the wicked..." (II Peter 2:4-7) very clearly indicates his agreement with Jude concerning the practices and attitudes of the inhabitants of Sodom.

A disregard for hospitality undoubtedly is poor manners, but it is hardly a sin that would receive such a denunciation from the Lord. As one reads of Lot's actions in Gen. 19, it appears that Lot was a fine host to his two strange friends. He greeted them at the gate of the city and bowed himself before them with his face to the ground. (Gen. 19:1) He invited them into his servant's house to wash their feet, and then set before them a feast. (19:2) In fact, he even protects his guests by offering his daughters to the mob. The mob, of course, was composed of poor hosts, precisely because its members desired to commit acts of perversion upon Lot's guests. Note that it was the mob's acts of perversion that the Lord labeled as wicked. The terms "sin," "defilers of the flesh," etc., are descriptive of the mob in Sodom—a mob consisting of young and old perverts (Gen. 19:4).

Josephus, the Jewish historian, in his *Antiquities* clearly identified the sin of Sodom with homosexual practices. He wrote, "About this time the Sodomites were proud on account of their riches...they hated strangers and abused themselves with Sodomitical practices."

146

A Jewish midrash on Genesis commented, "The Sodomites made an agreement among themselves, that whenever a stranger visited them, they should force him to sodomy and rob him of his money." [29]

Clement of Alexandria stated that the Sodomites had "fallen into uncleanliness, practicing adultery shamelessly and burning with insane love for boys." [30]

And Augustine wrote in his *Apostolic Constitution,* "Thou shalt not corrupt boys, for this wickedness is contrary to nature and arose from Sodom." [31]

## Moses and Homosexuality

Following the giving of the Mosaic Law, the Scriptures continue to press hard on the sin of homosexuality. Moses says, "Thou shalt not lie with mankind, as with womankind, it is abomination." (Lev. 18:22), and "if a man also lie with mankind, as he lieth with a woman, both of them have committed an abomination, they will surely be put to death, their blood shall be upon them." (Lev. 20:13)

Of course, some homosexuals try to soften Moses' blow by arguing that other Biblical characters had homosexual relationships. The ones usually cited are Ruth and Naomi, David and Jonathan, Paul and Timothy and Jesus and John.

Troy Perry, founder of the Sodomy Church (later renamed the Metropolitan Community Church) states that he does not believe that Jesus was a homosexual but continued by saying, "Here was a guy that was raised by a mother with no father—typical of the homosexual syndrome...he never married and ran around with twelve guys all the time. Not only that. He wasn't above bodily contact with another man: John the Beloved lay on the breast of Jesus at the Last Supper. Not only that, but a guy betrayed him with a kiss." [33]

John Boswell certainly tried to hint that Jesus and John were lovers in one of his paintings entitled "Christ and St. John." Says Boswell, "This very sentimental representation of an older Christ and a youthful Saint John is strongly evocative of the tradition of passionate friendship common among the monastic clergy of the Middle Ages and romanticized earlier by writers like Saint Aebred of Rievaulx." [34]

Since practicing homosexuals are obsessed with sex and place their sexuality before family, friends and even God, they obviously read into Biblical passages homosexual acts that just are not there.

Typical of such obsession is the sixty-six line poem by English professor James Kirkup, entitled, "The Love that Dares to Speak His Name." The poem purports to describe the feeling of a homosexual Roman Centurion toward Christ after his body had been taken from the cross.

According to *Christianity Today* (Aug. 12, 1977, p. 34), some pleaded that the poem was intended to express love for Christ—though it was love not in the normal heterosexual sense, but in the homosexual sense.

Such abominations are only possible through a sex-obsessed personality who sees and feels and gives sexual meaning to all events. Only a homosexual could read the story of Ruth and come up with the conclusion that Ruth and Naomi were lesbians. The same is true in the case of David and Jonathan.

The Scriptural commentary on David's life has no such sin laid to his account. The Lord says David's sins were murder and adultery (I Kings 15:5), not homosexuality. Homosexuality is sexual lust, not soul love.

Besides, the very context of I Kings 15:5 rules out the conjecture that David was homosexual. In the previous chapter (I Kings 14), the Lord mentions the evilness of Rehoboam for allowing the Sodomites to practice their abominations in the land (I Kings 14:21-24), and, a few years later, King Asa is praised for taking away "the Sodomites out of the land" (I Kings 14:11, 12). Had David been guilty of homosexuality, it would have been mentioned and condemned.

King Josiah, likewise, did that which was right in the sight of the Lord, and he broke down the houses of the Sodomites (II Kings 23:7).

On the other side of the coin when we are told, for example, that Rehoboam "did evil in the sight of the Lord" we are immediately told that "there were also sodomites in the land: and they did according to all the abominations of the nations which the Lord cast out before the children of Israel." (I Kings 14:22, 24)

The "abominations of the nations" is a reference to Leviticus 18:3 where the Lord instructs Moses and the nation of Israel not to walk in the depraved ways of Egypt and Canaan. The ways of these nations are a defilement, iniquity and an abomination to God (Lev. 18:24, 25). The Lord says to Moses, "Defile not ye yourselves in any of these things." What things?

The Lord lists five "abominable customs" (Lev. 18:30) he does not want Israel to practice: (1) incest (Lev. 18:6f) (2) adultery (Lev. 18:20), (3) infanticide (Lev. 18:21), (4) homosexuality (Lev. 18:22), and (5) bestiality (Lev. 18:23). Says the Lord, "For all these abominations have the men of the land done, which were before you, and the land is defiled" (Lev. 18:27).

And again, "Ye shall not walk in the manners of the nations, which I cast out before you: for they committed all these things, and therefore I abhorred them" (Lev. 20:23).

When Israel finally fell to the Assyrians in 722/21 B.C. the reasons for her fall recorded in II Kings 17 were walking in the immoral customs of Egypt and Canaan doing "secretly those things that were not right against the Lord their God" (II Kings 17:9).

149

Isaiah makes it very clear that homosexuality was one of those "secret things." Says Isaiah, "Except the Lord of hosts had left unto us a very small remnant, we should have been as Sodom and Gomorrah" (Isaiah 1:9). In fact, Isaiah refers to the government of Israel as "rulers of Sodom" and to the population as "ye people of Gomorrah" (Isaiah 1:10). Instead of avoiding the unnatural lusts and evil customs of Egypt and Canaan Israel adopted their depravities and likewise lost their land.

And Jeremiah leaves little doubt as to why Judah went into the Babylonian captivity some one hundred thirty-six years later. "I have seen also in the prophets of Jerusalem a horrible thing: they commit adultery, and walk in lies, they strengthen also the hands of evildoers that none doth return from his wickedness: they are all of them unto me as Sodom, and the inhabitants thereof as Gomorrah." (Jer. 23:14)

Yet modern writers are calling for "the adoption of new attitudes towards acts prohibited in the past." [35] According to Seton Hall University's Associate Professor of Religious Studies, Michael F. Valente, fornication, homosexuality, and bestiality are part of a new sexual ethic. This new ethic rejects the past approach to sexual ethics and allows shepherds "sexual release with their sheep" [36] and prisoners homosexual liaisons. With our new world view, new attitudes, and new ethics we can no longer declare certain acts as "intrinsically evil and always gravely serious if they do not conform to a specific concept of 'nature.'" [37] In other words, homosexuality and bestiality are moral!

The Rev. Neale Secor exclaims, "What Christian interested in the future of situational-relational ethics can help but breathe a sigh of ecclesiastical relief—at last, liberation from twenty-five long centuries of Levitical world view." [38] Instead of basing our ethics on the myths

150

of Scripture it is important to accept what the social scientists, cultural historians, anthropologists and modern day investigators are saying about homosexuality. Secor feels that anthropological studies lend support to the idea that "society itself and not the homosexual basically is the 'sick' patient." [39]

Not surprising, Letha Scanzoni and Virginia Mollenkott follow the same line of reasoning to obtain their particular conclusion regarding homosexuality. "Since the Bible is silent about the homosexual condition," say the two authors, "those who want to understand it must rely on the findings of modern behavioral science research." [40] Following voodoo hermeneutics (e.g., "It should be noted that some Bible scholars do not believe that the intent of the men of Sodom was sexual" [41] and "we are forced to admit that the Sodom story says nothing at all about the homosexual condition" [42]); and weird illustrations (e.g., two homosexuals "found great joy in sexually celebrating their love on Saturday night and then kneeling side by side the next morning to take Holy Communion together" [43]) Scanzoni and Mollenkott cleverly neutralize every Scriptural injunction against homosexuality in order to reach their conclusion of "stable, monogamous relationships among homosexuals." [44] Thankfully, however, they do note that "perhaps it is wise to keep pedophiles or pederasts from teaching children." [45]

## Christ and Homosexuality

The New Testament does not give the homosexual any more reasons to cheer. The one big difference between the Old and New Testaments lies in the fact that under the Old Testament dispensation the homosexuals were either executed or exiled, while under the New Testament, the homosexual is to be warned that his activity is sinful and under the wrath of God (Romans 1:18-27);

and that if he is a member of the local Christian assembly, he is to be dismissed (I Cor. 5:6). However, some insist that, since Jesus Christ never specifically mentioned such perversion, Christ was soft on homosexuality.

The obvious reply to such an insinuation is found in the following facts: (a) Christ's very positive statement in Mark 10:6f., "But from the beginning of creation God made them *male and female*. For this cause shall a man leave his father and mother, and *cleave to his wife,* and the two shall be one flesh." Male and female, says Christ, were created for each other, since the only meaningful and holy sexual relationship is the male-female relationship.

(b) In Luke 17:28f, our Lord warns his disciples about the moral climate of the endtime and says, "Likewise also as it was in the days of Lot . . . the same day that Lot went out of Sodom it rained fire and brimstone from heaven, and destroyed them all."

Not only will homosexuality characterize the endtime as it characterized the endtime of Sodom, but the Antichrist himself could well be a homosexual. In Daniel's description of the anti-Christ, he says, "Neither shall he regard the God of his fathers, *nor the desire of women,* nor regard any god, for he shall magnify himself above all." (Dan. 11:37) Homosexuals not only have an aversion to human conception and to marital fidelity, but also they have a marked tendency toward feelings of moral superiority.

(c) Matthew 19:9 records, "Whosoever shall put away his wife, except it be for fornication, and shall marry another, committeth adultery." The Greek word for fornication is *porneia* and means giving one's self to unlawful sexual relationship. The word is used in Jude 1:7 in reference to Sodom and Gomorrah's sins of immorality, i.e., homosexuality. The term fornication or *porneia* certainly includes homosexuality, and Christ said it is a sin that indeed severs the marriage bond.

Our Lord Jesus Christ, therefore, does have a good deal to say about the subject of homosexuality; so does the Apostle Paul. Indeed, Paul turns out to be the arch-nemesis of the gay community. Few pastors in the Metropolitan Community Church preach with conviction from Paul's writings in Romans, I Cor. 6 and I Tim. 1. In fact, the homosexuals refer to him as "asexual" Paul. But what Paul condemns is illicit sexual relationships—never godly relationships. Paul, who authored the three previously mentioned books of the New Testament, is thought by many scholars to have penned these words in Hebrews, "Marriage is honorable in all, and the bed undefiled, but fornicators (including homosexuals) and adulterers God will judge." (Heb. 13:4)

## Gays Against Nature

Romans I has to be the New Testament paradigm on homosexuality. There, Paul condemns both male and female (lesbian) homosexuality as he says, "For this cause God gave them up unto vile affections, for even their women did change the natural use into that which is against nature's law. And likewise also the men, leaving the natural use of the woman, burned in their lust one toward another, men with men working that which is unseemly, and receiving in themselves that recompense of their error which was meet." (Rom. 1:26, 27)

We have yet to see a good explanation of these two verses from a homosexual point of view! Some of them seek to play down the importance of Paul's writings by saying that Christ is the founder of Christianity and that, therefore, we should stick with the red-letter edition of the Bible. If that be the case, hopefully they will read carefully Matt. 19, Mark 10 and Luke 17.

153

Others say that Paul cannot be referring to present day "psychological" homosexuals since he did not have access to the science of psychology and sociology. Such distinctions are beside the point. It is the act itself that Paul condemns. It is "men working with men that which is unseemly" that Paul addresses. A practicing modern-day homosexual falls under the condemning words of Paul just as forcefully as did a first-century invert or pervert. A psychological invert, in practice, performs the same detestable acts as a heterosexual pervert. Both have left the natural use of the woman and both burn in their lusts one toward another.

But to make sure he does not ignore any different kinds of sexual perverts, Paul condemns both the passive (Gr. *malakoi*) and the active homosexual (Gr. *arsenokoitai*) in I Cor. 6:9 and states that such unrighteousness "shall not inherit the kingdom of God." Even the Revised Standard Version, copyrighted by the National Council of Churches, translates I Cor. 6:9 as "homosexuals," and the latter Greek word *arsenokoitai* might even be translated to mean "an obsessive corruption of boys." This verse certainly seems to contradict the modern-day theologian quoted earlier who said that homosexual acts "may not be interpreted as excluding one from the domain of God's gracious intention." Paul says such behavior surely does exclude one from the Kingdom of God.

To make sure that no one misreads his earlier comments on the subject, Paul again sets forth his case in I Tim. 1:9, 10. The law, he says, is not for the righteous, but is for the ungodly, for sinners, for unholy and profane, for murderers, for whoremongers, for homosexuals, for kidnappers, for liars.

This leaves us in a quandary over Rev. G. William Sheek's previously mentioned comment that the Bible does not have a consistently clear stand on the subject of homosexuality, when, in fact, the Bible clearly takes a consistent stand on the subject. From Genesis to Revelation homosexuality is treated as sin and "exceeding wickedness."

To speak of "good gay Christians" is a contradiction in terms. True repentance includes the forsaking of sin. The Bible says, "He that covereth his sins shall not prosper, but whoso confesseth and forsaketh them shall have mercy." (Prov. 28:13)

Although many defenders of homosexuality contend that most homosexuals do not wish to change their lifestyle, there are, in fact, some who desire to change. On the basis of I Cor. 6:9-11 those who desire to change may have full assurance from God that He will wash, sanctify and justify penitent sinners in the name of the Lord Jesus by the Spirit of God.

Since God is in the business of saving sinners, the absolute minimum requirement asked of the homosexual is to accept God's view of the homosexual life-style, admitting that it is what God calls it—sin.

Obviously, a homosexual cannot expect God to save or deliver him from his predicament if he continues to view his problem as the result of kinky genes or of a chromosomal quirk. The Lord does not desire to hear someone other than the guilty party receive the blame. For a very interesting graphic illustration of this truth, observe C.S. Lewis' portrayal of Napoleon written in his book *The Great Divorce*. Napoleon is pictured in hell in the following words:

"Walking up and down, up and down all the time—left-right, left-right—never stopping for a moment. The two chaps watched him for about a year and he never rested. And muttering to himself all the time, 'It was Soult's fault. It was Ney's fault. It was Josephine's fault. It was the fault of the Russians. It was the fault of the English.' Like that all the time."

Many homosexuals live their lives just as Lewis portrays Napoleon—blaming everyone but themselves.

## There Is Deliverance

Therefore, the first thing a homosexual must do is to agree with God that his homosexual life-style is sin. Obviously, if it were not sinful, the homosexual would not need to be saved from it.

But if a homosexual (male or female) is willing to call his desire sin, then there exists a Saviour who God has graciously provided willing to save the sinner and to deliver him from his spiritual and physical infirmity—our Lord Jesus Christ.

The Bible makes it very clear that Christ came to seek and to save that which was lost (Luke 19:10) and that He gave His life as ransom for sin that we might enjoy eternal life as His gift.

This is the meaning of such passages, as, "But as many as received him, to them gave he power to become the sons of God" (John 1:12); "Believe on the Lord Jesus Christ, and thou shalt be saved" (Acts 16:31); or "That if thou shalt believe in thine heart that God hath raised him from the dead, thou shalt be saved." (Rom. 10:9)

Although many homosexuals feel the apostle Paul is their worst enemy, he is indeed their best friend. For one thing, Paul was not afraid to tell the homosexual the truth, but another important item involves Paul's specific commission. Paul's mission was to be a minister and a witness of the Lord "to open their eyes and to turn them from darkness to light, and from the power of Satan unto God, that they may receive forgiveness of sins and inheritance among them which are sanctified by faith that is in Me . . . that they should repent and turn to God and do works meet for repentance." (Acts 26:16—20)

Every penitent homosexual will find that Christ's salvation is sufficient—powerful enough to free him from his life-style of sin.

1. Enrique T. Rueda, *The Homosexual Network*, p. 248.
2. *Christianity Today*, December 17, 1982, p. 50.
3. *Ibid.*
4. *Ibid.*
5. *Ibid.*, April 22, 1983, p. 8.
6. *Ibid.*
7. *Ibid.*
8. *Ibid.*
9. *Newsweek*, October 11, 1982, p. 113.
10. *Time*, October 11, 1982, p. 67.
11. Rueda, *op. cit.*, p. 270.
12. *Ibid.*
13. *Time*, May 23, 1983, p. 58.
14. *Ibid.*
15. *Ibid.*
16. Rueda, *op. cit.*, p. 276.
17. *Ibid.*
18. *Ibid.*, p. 277.
19. *Ibid.*, p. 343.
20. *Ibid.*, p. 260.
21. *Ibid.*, p. 368.
22. *Ibid.*, p. 249.
23. *United Press International*, October 25, 1980.
24. Rueda, *op. cit.*, p. 246.
25. *United Press International*, October 25, 1980.
26. John J. McNeill, *The Church and the Homosexual*, p. 46.
27. John Boswell, *Christianity, Social Tolerance, and Homosexuality*, p. 93.
28. Tom Horner, *Jonathan Loved David: Homosexuality in Biblical Times* (Philadelphia: The Westminster Press, 1978), p. 48.
29. *Gen. Rabbah* 50.7 per *the Church and the Homosexual*, p. 74.
30. *Paed.*, iii 8 per *Ibid.*
31. *Apostolic Constitution*, vii. 2 per *Ibid.*
32. John W. Drakeford, *A Christian View of Homosexuality*, p. 25.
33. Troy Perry and Charles L. Lucas, *The Lord Is My Shepherd And He Knows I'm Gay* (Los Angeles: Nash Publisher, Inc., 1972), p. 152.
34. John Boswell, *op. cit.*, painting across from page 207.
35. Edward Batchelor, Jr., *Homosexuality and Ethics*, p. 153.

36. *Ibid.*, p. 151.
37. *Ibid.*, p. 153.
38. *Ibid.*, p. 155.
39. *Ibid.*, p. 162.
40. Letha Scanzoni and Virginia Mollenkott, *Is the Homosexual My Neighbor,* p. 71.
41. *Ibid.*, p. 55.
42. *Ibid.*, p. 59.
43. *Ibid.*, p. 63.
44. *Ibid.*, p. 126.
45. *Ibid.*, p. 97.

Conclusion

*"If God doesn't judge America, he'll owe
Sodom and Gomorrah an apology."*
                              *—Mrs. Billy Graham*

In concluding our study of the homosexual revolution, a number of trends are apparent. The most current is that of the new homosexual quest for recognition by society. The homosexual no longer wishes to be part of a sub-culture. Like the marijuana smoker, the homosexual wants society to label his activity "acceptable."

Only a society with a "death wish" would consent to such a demand. As George Gilder observes, "Bad sex drives out good, and, worst of all, philandering and homosexuality are exalted. Gay liberation, pornographic glut and one-night trysts are all indices of sexual frustration; all usually disclose a failure to achieve profound and loving sexuality. When a society deliberately affirms these failures—*contemplates legislation of homosexual marriage,* celebrates the women who denounce the family, and indulges pornography as a manifestation of sexual health and a release from repression—the culture is promoting a form of erotic suicide. It is destroying the cultural preconditions of profound love and sexuality: the durable heterosexual relationships necessary to a community of emotional investments and continuities in which children can find a secure place."[1]

And there is no doubt that the homosexual movement is out to redefine the family. Father-mother-child must give way to a new definition which will include homosexual marriages, adoptions, and even artificial insemination. Prof. James B. Nelson put it like this, "Because of their sexual orientations, gay folk appear to disvalue commonly-held values concerning marriage, family and children."[2]

Enrique Rueda says it was in early 1970 when the homosexual movement identified the family as harmful to its interests, and said its goal was: "The abolition of the nuclear family because it perpetuates the false categories of homosexuality and heterosexuality."[3] In a lesbian workshop the feminists were told, "The nuclear family is a microcosm of the fascist state, where the women and children are owned by, and their fates determined by, the needs of men in a man's world."[4]

Though 1970 vintage, it sounds strikingly similar to 1982 thinking on our campuses where *Newsweek* reports: "Others say that they are lesbians for political as well as personal reasons. The most radical lesbians *report heterosexuality* as the oppression of a male-dominated society."[5]

Nevertheless, the homosexual community is using numerous legal and psychological maneuverings to bring such a situation to pass.

The one powerful weapon being employed by the homosexual hierarchy today consists of the placement of the homosexual movement within the confines of the black struggle for civil rights. The homosexual is seeking to make his quest for civil rights (the right to employment, housing, etc.) appear analogous to the black's quest for employment and housing.

Most people certainly realize, however, that employing a black to teach in the classroom is far from being analogous to employing a homosexual to teach. *Time* magazine acknowledged that "though strategically effective, the analogy with blacks surely begs the question of whether homosexuality is as irrelevant and accidental as skin color."[6]

## Gays/Trans/Fetish

The cold, hard, irrefutable fact is that homosexuality has no more legitimate claims to the civil rights movement than has transvestism, fetishism, voyeurism, pedophilia, exhibitionism, necrophilia, sadism, masochism and bestiality. All such aberrant social behavior must be contained, segregated, controlled and stigmatized.

If the homosexual is allowed to teach grade school children that "gay is good" and high schoolers that "the revolution of free and frequent polysexuality" is sophisticated, then who is going to object when the transvestite asks to be given equal time to sell his pancake make-up to school children?

Does the panderer of the dead (necrophiliac) have a right to explain to our children the thrills of making love to dead people? Rock musician Alice Cooper exploits necrophilia in his song "Cold Ethyl" and "I Love The Dead." In "I Love The Dead," he sings, "I never even knew your now rotting face." Should he be given equal time in the classroom?

Does the sadist have the right to explain his rope tricks or the exhibitionist the right to display his private parts? Already the homosexuals are preparing the way for transvestite civil rights. Peter Fisher, in his *Gay Mystique,* writes, "Transvestites, leather and S and M people are no longer looked upon as the outcasts of the gay world—their insights into our society and its sexual roles are highly valued...you can admire a transvestite who achieves a rare beauty and grace because she is proud to be herself." [7]

Unless we are completely insane, the answer to all the above questions obviously is, "No!" Children are our most precious gifts from the Lord and parents have an obligation before God to raise their children up in the nurture and admonition of the Lord. If state or federal government looses the homosexuals, transvestites, sadists, masochists, pederasts and other deviants on our children (as is now being done in those states where homosexuals are teaching sex education courses), then Christians will be forced to choose the option mentioned by the Apostle Peter, "We ought to obey God rather than men." (Acts 5:29)

Unfortunately, the expression "sexual orientation" as found in the 1980 Democratic National Convention platform includes all of the above aberrant sexual behavior. Its plank doesn't just condone sexual acts between consenting adult males or females. In fact, as one might recall, the 1972 Gay Rights Platform doesn't mention "consenting adults." It calls for the repeal of law prohibiting private sexual acts involving "consenting persons." When the Democratic National Committee calls for the elimination of "all laws, rules and regulations which discriminate against individuals (notice, not adults) on the basis of sexual orientation" Pandora's Box is wide open. The pederast certainly is covered under such a broad umbrella as "sexual orientation." But then so is the transvestite, sadist, masochist. The Washington, D.C. Act 4-69 even found room under its "sexual orientation" provisions for bestiality.

In reality, there is no end to the shameful acts against nature sanctioned by the expression "sexual orientation." To make this expression the law of the land (as the Federal Gay Rights Bill would do) is to invite every depraved, perverted weirdo out of the woodwork and into federal employment. Washington would approach Sodom and Gomorrah.

It should be clear to all that the forces opposed to homosexuality did not start this fight. Jean O'Leary of the National Gay Task Force issued the following statement obviously designed with potential press coverage rather than truth in mind: "We were forced into the battle with Anita Bryant. We did not seek it." Such statements are simply not true. The first thousand punches were thrown by the organized homosexuals in their move to gain equal or preferred treatment under the law. If heterosexuals can teach in the schools and glorify male-female relationships, the homosexuals insist they want equal time to glorify male/male or lesbian relationships. If the heterosexuals can operate schools for boys, the homosexuals want equal opportunity, too.

We have tried to present, to the best of our ability, the homosexual scene and the revolution that has ensued. We believe that this revolution must be met head on and decisively challenged.

It certainly is not a human rights or civil rights issue, unless one is willing to make other forms of aberrant behavior civil rights issues.

The homosexual revolution is definitely a moral issue, an issue on which we all must take a firm stand, remembering that "the only thing necessary for the triumph of evil is for good men to do nothing."

Therefore, we are suggesting that the following positive steps be taken in order to challenge and contain the homosexual menace:

Parents must be alerted to the ever-increasing incidence of homosexual activity, so that they might sufficiently teach their children concerning the dangers inherent in it. Each child must be instructed to report to his parents any homosexual advances—whether these advances be made in a YMCA, a Boy Scout or Girl Scout troop, a school or church.

One reason young people get trapped in long homosexual relationships is that, once seduced, they are afraid to tell their parents. In fact, the homosexual seducer cautions his victims never to tell anyone. Young people need to be told not to be afraid to report homosexual advances. It is not sinful to be the victim of planned seduction, but it is sinful to continue a homosexual relationship in silence. If youthful victims would take immediate action, a great deal of homosexual activity would be "cut off at the pass."

Parents, once informed by their children of having been seduced, should take immediate action. They should contact the morals squad of their local police department, their district attorney or their local sheriff's department. If a child was seduced in a YMCA, Scout troop, school or church, the parents should contact the head of the organization and ask for a full investigation. These organizations will move quickly—they cannot afford to remain silent. Their very existence depends on their willingness and ability to protect the rights of children from homosexual abuse.

In turn, these organizations, after conducting a thorough investigation, should write up a full report on the matter, dismiss the offending employee, report to the police and insure that any future employer of the homosexual offender is aware of his activity. One telling sin of some churches is to dismiss their pastor for homosexual activity but never alert his next church of his past activity. Invariably, the next church discovers that the pastor has not put an end to recruiting children for his nefarious purposes.

Ministers of the Gospel must take to their pulpits and proclaim to their congregations the Biblical message regarding homosexuality. America no longer can afford the luxury of a silent clergy that chooses to ignore an activity so evil that God has destroyed nations and cities in order to contain it.

In times past America's clergy have been eager to proclaim the truth that no political act can be right if it is morally wrong. To declare homosexuality politically and culturally right when it is so obviously morally wrong is a sure road to destruction.

Clergymen, therefore, have the obligation to proclaim homosexuality as sin—a part of man's old nature.

They must instruct their church members on the necessity of living the normal Spirit-filled Christian life. "If ye then be risen with Christ, seek those things which are above, where Christ sitteth on the right hand of God." (Col. 3:1)

A new day will dawn in this nation when the clergy again speak of Biblical moral absolutes and expose the abominations of paganism.

Ministers of local churches within major denominations must be made aware of the slanted "study documents" offered them from their denominational headquarters. These studies usually carry disclaimers like "it is a study document only," or "it is not to be construed as an official statement of attitudes or policies." In fact, the study drips with "attitude" and is intended to slant policy in favor of the homosexual life-style.

The minister and local church are told that there is a "spareness" of Biblical teaching on the subject of homosexuality or that there are "only eleven passages" in the whole Bible dealing with the subject. The truth is that all eleven passages condemn homosexuality. Surely eleven clear-cut passages should be more than sufficient to know God's will toward this perversion.

The sleight-of-hand tactics used by denominational leaders bent on seeing homosexuals accepted by the local churches are clever: (a) Denounce those taking a stand against homosexuals as "judgmental," (b) Insist that those opposed to homosexuals lack sufficient data, reason, sensitivity and knowledge of the whole issue, (c) Twist and downgrade the teaching of Scripture, e.g., that Sodom's sin is inhospitality; or that Paul merely condemns homosexuals involved in cultic, pagan or idolatrous rites; or that Jesus never deals with the subject of homosexuality, (d) Insist that recent scientific studies prove "X" percent of the population engages in homosexual acts. This reasoning insists that, since a percentage of the population is homosexual in its sexual and

167

affectional orientation, the act must be accepted by way of submerging it under the "love" implication of the Gospel of Christ.

Denominational study documents, though giving the air of completeness, say little or nothing about homosexual life-styles, seduction techniques, molestation of children, homosexual crime and venereal disease.

Most Christians will reject homosexuality on the basis of God's Word and because of the homosexual's bizarre, perverted life-style. Therefore, it is important to place this study in the hand of local ministers in order to complete their understanding of homosexuality.

Each citizen must become informed about and opposed to local, state and federal legislation favorable to the homosexual revolution. For example, state laws proscribing sodomy and crimes against nature should remain intact and should be vigorously enforced. Federal government actions to legitimize homosexuality should be opposed. House and Senate legislation seeking to make homosexuality a matter of civil rights should be opposed.

Each State of the United States should place before the voters of the State an initiative petition allowing the citizens of each state to vote yes or not on whether or not the voters of the State desire that homosexuals teach, administer, or counsel children.

Such action would send our message to Washington. The inevitable result would be a slow-down on hiring of homosexuals for federal jobs and, even more importantly, it would put a tremendous dent in the homosexuals' recruiting program. The size of the next generation of homosexuals would be drastically reduced if their breeding grounds were dried up.

Citizens must voice their opinion regarding the placement of homosexuals in critical national security positions.

Concerned citizens should protest the proposed "gay" rights plank in the 1984 Democratic Party and Republican Party platforms, and voice strong objections toward any soft-on-homosexual stance. If enough citizens protested, the homosexual revolution would be set back many years.

Ad hoc committees should be formed since these committees give parents the strength of a collective voice to protect their children. Responsible Citizens of America, P.O. Box 207, Manitou Springs, CO 80829, Moral Majority, 499 S. Capitol, Washington, D.C. 20003, Concerned Women for America, P.O. Box 20376, El Cajon, CA 92021 or Eagle Forum, Box 618, Alton, Illinois 62002 are all excellent groups worth joining, supporting, and /or encouraging.

Tim LaHaye's book *The Battle for the Mind* gives numerous concrete examples of the effectiveness of these ad hoc committees. One involved the Human Relations Committee recommendation to the Santa Clara County Board of Supervisors to strike down all laws regarding discrimination on the basis of sexual choice. Church people banded together, gathered 50,000 signatures in two weeks, and placed the issue on the ballot.

Church women's groups, service clubs, parent-teacher associations, Big Brothers, Boy Scout and Girl Scout organizations and other groups should be enlisted in this struggle as quickly as possible. They all have much to lose if the homosexuals win the struggle to have access to their youth.

Parents should write letters to the editor of their newspapers in order to keep militant homosexuals on the defensive and make sure that the networks and government leaders know that grassroots America cares about moral standards.

Our nation must be alerted to the tremendous moral, social, and political ramifications of the homosexual revolution. The materials in this book will help convince most honest thinking people that homosexuality is not an alternative life style, not even a civil rights issue, but rather a moral issue.

The homosexual sub-culture has absolutely nothing to commend itself for acceptance in civilized society. It is a negation of God's order; can never be an ideal 'family' or 'education' model; is a parasite on heterosexual society; is a negation of pro-creative life; is a cesspool of communicable disease and is a gross cop-out, ignoring the parental responsibility that God originally expected men and women to bear. It destroys lives, families, institutions, and nations.

In Loomis' *Gay Spirit,* he says that homosexuals do not have to contend with "pregnancy, diaphragms, daily hat compliments, marriage contracts and divorce settlement, alimony, babies that screech in the night and adultery."

Loomis just defined homosexuality! It is a negation of God's design for a productive life. When a nation allows homosexuality to negate marriage, pregnancy, and babies—that nation already has committed genocide. Loomis can be thankful that his parents had no such philosophy.

The homosexual revolution is an explosive issue. The battle lines are being drawn. It is either back, back, back to the standards of the Word of God, or it is on, on, on to atheism, sodomy, totalitarianism and despair.

It will take committed action by every Christian to bring this country back to the traditional moral standards of the Word of God.

1. George Gilder, *Sexual Suicide,* p. 4, 5.
2. Edward Batchelor, Jr., *Homosexuality and Ethics,* p. 205.
3. Enrique T. Rueda, *The Homosexual Network,* p. 221.
4. *Ibid.*
5. *Newsweek,* April 5, 1982, p. 76.

6. *Time,* September 8, 1975, p. 36.

7. Peter Fisher, *The Gay Mystique,* p. 229.

8. See Rueda, *The Homosexual Network,* Chapter 9 for a detailed account of "The Funding of the Homosexual Movement."

Glossary

*"That degenerate will put us all back ten thousand years with her foul deeds at Butt's Crematorium."*

*—The Queen's Vernacular*

The following glossary of terms is derived primarily from the authoritative homosexual lexicon, Bruce Rodger's *The Queen's Vernacular* (San Francisco: Straight Arrow Books, 1972). The lexicon contains over 12,000 entries, most of which are not fit for decent conversation. *The Queen's Vernacular* certainly reinforces Jude's description of homosexuals as "filthy dreamers" (Jude 1:7, 8). It also confirms the fact that homosexuals do seduce and molest youth. Such acts are written implicitly into homosexual figures of speech, e.g., chicken, chicken queen, chicken freak, chicken hawk, vampire, etc.

"The uses of what most people consider vulgar language," says Enrique T. Rueda, "pervades the homosexual literature and even otherwise 'serious' publications. Likewise, the practice of 'camp' by a large number of homosexuals constitutes an almost distinctive feature of the homosexual culture." [1]

**Adonis,** perfect specimen of male physique.
**Alice,** the police.
**Auntie,** a middle-aged homosexual.
**B and D,** bondage and discipline. Sexual excitement related to binding or being bound by rope, handcuffs, leather, etc.

**Baby Butch,** adolescent lesbian.

**Bar,** public locale (bar, bench) where men gather for sex.

**Bat,** a homosexual.

**Batch Night,** two homosexual "lovers" cruising for separate sexual encounters.

**Bath House,** sometimes called church, den of sin, flesh factory, skin room or the tubs. Place where bathing is secondary, sex is primary.

**Batter,** a male prostitute.

**Beads,** gayness.

**Bean Queen,** Mexican homosexual.

**Belly Queen,** a homosexual attracted to stomachs for sexual purposes.

**Benny House,** a bordello featuring young boys for homosexual purposes.

**Bestiality,** the practice of having sexual relations between a person and an animal.

**Big Bertha,** nickname for an effeminate, tall, heavy-set man.

**Big Game,** one who is stalked for future seduction.

**Bisexual,** one who is sexually interested in both men and women. Also referred to as AC-DC, ambidextrous, ambisextrous, bi, bicycle, convertible, flippy, gray cat, side saddle queen, switch-hitter, two-way baby.

**Bitch,** an insolent, resentful homosexual.

**Black Widow,** male homosexual who habitually steals love-mates of other homosexuals.

**Bondage Queen,** one who receives sexual pleasure through the practice of being tied up, humiliated, raped.

**Brown Family,** the homosexual sub-culture.

**Brownie Queen,** a passive partner.

**Buckaruby,** a homosexual cowboy.

**Buddy,** the homosexual love-mate.

**Bull,** an aggressive lesbian.

**Butch,** a lesbian with masculine characteristics.

**Bullring,** brothel of male prostitutes.

**Chicken,** male under the age of consent.

**Chicken Dinner,** sex with a teenager.

**Chicken Freak,** elderly man with a sexual appetite for young men.

**Chicken Hawk,** older man whose lust peculiarities are shared solely with young boys. (Also called chicken hunter, chicken queen, coke-roller.)

**Clean Queen,** a homosexual cruising at a laundromat.

**Closet Queen,** a homosexual who is afraid to reveal his homosexuality.

**Coffin Queen,** one who takes sexual interest in corpses (see necrophilism)

**Creature,** a drug-taking, long-haired homosexual.

**Cruise,** the practice of looking for sex. (see Troll)

**Dangle Queen,** a gay exhibitionist.

**Degenerate,** a homosexual lacking the respect of his peers primarily because of his participation in gross sex acts, e.g., necrophilism.

**Dinge Queen,** white homosexual who prefers black men.

**Drag,** wearing clothing of the opposite sex.

**Dyke,** a mannish lesbian.

**Eclair Queen,** a rich homosexual.

**Effie,** an effeminate homosexual.

**Egyptian Queen,** a black male homosexual.

**Exhibitionism,** the practice of exposing one's sexual organs for sexual gratification.

**Fag,** male homosexual.

**Fairy,** an effeminate homosexual.

**Femme,** a passive lesbian.

**Fetishism,** the arousal of sexual feelings by non-sexual objects, e.g., leather, urine, etc.

**Flash Queen,** gay drug pusher.

**Fluff,** effeminate homosexual.

**Forbidden Fruit,** homosexual infested with V.D.

**Freak,** a homosexual.

**Fruit,** any male homosexual.

**Fruit fly,** a women who likes to associate with male homosexuals.

**Gay,** homosexual.

**Gay Chicken,** a homosexual teenager.

**Golden Queen,** a homosexual sexually aroused by urine.

**Greek,** an active pederast.

**Hermaphrodite,** one born with the genitals of both sexes.

**Himmer,** male homosexual.

**Homosexual,** one who engages in acts of a sexual nature with member's of one's own sex. Usually includes mutual masturbation, anal, and oral sex. (See Belly Queen, etc.)

**Hungry,** a promiscuous homosexual.

**Husband,** the dominant masculine homosexual in a gay marriage.

**Hustler,** a male prostitute.

**Ladder,** older male homosexual, desiring young boys. (see Chicken Hawk)

**Lavender,** color symbol for homosexuality.

**Leather,** a frequent fetish object of homosexuals who participate in sado-masochistic acts.

**Lesbian,** a female homosexual. (see also Sappho)

**Lilly,** the police.

**Madam,** mature homosexual man.

**Mame,** one who assumes the wife position in a gay marriage.

**Masochism,** the practice of receiving sexual gratification from being dominated, mistreated, or hurt by one's sex partner.

**Maso-sissy,** masochistic homosexual man.

**Menu,** toilet wall lined with graffiti.

**Misogyny,** hatred of women.

**Model,** a male prostitute.

**Molly Dyke,** the passive lesbian.

**Mom,** lesbian who plays up her femininity.

178

**Mother,** one who introduces another to homosexual activity.

**Nelly,** effeminate queer.

**Ophelia,** a gay hippy.

**Pansy,** male homosexual.

**Panty Queen,** one who has a fetish for women's underwear.

**Pederasty,** homosexual acts between a man and a boy.

**Pedophilia,** obsessive sexual desire for children.

**Pig Pie,** a homosexual orgy, group sex.

**Pot Pie,** gay hippy.

**Queen,** a male homosexual.

**Queen Bee,** wealthy woman who surrounds herself with young homosexual men.

**Queen of Sheba,** a black homosexual.

**Queer,** a male homosexual.

**Railroad Queen,** homosexual who cruises hobo jungles.

**Read,** to recognize other homosexuals.

**Red-hot Mama,** a young homosexual.

**Ribbon Clerk,** a homosexual with a desk job.

**Rubber Queen,** homosexual with a rubber fetish, i.e., one who is turned on sexually by rubber garments.

**Sappho,** a lesbian. Sappho was a Greek poetess who lived on the island of Lesbos in the 7th to 6th centuries, B.C. Some of her poetry expresses her passionate love for other women.

**San Francisco Faggot,** self-acclaimed heterosexual who really likes boys. (Also leather queens and hustlers.)

**Shaker,** homosexual loitering in front of a urinal.

**Showgirl,** a homosexual showoff.

**Sissy,** the effeminate homosexual or passive homosexual male.

**Sister,** male homosexual befriended by lesbians.

**Sixty-nine,** the practice of homosexuals engaging in mutual oral sex.

**S and M,** sadism and masochism. Sexual pleasure derived from fetishes, pain, torture, etc. (see maso-chism).

**Snack Bar,** homosexual club offering its members a large orgy room for group sex.

**Sodom,** any place with a large percentage of male homosexuals.

**Sofa Case,** an insecure homosexual.

**Soiree,** social affair given by and for homosexuals.

**Sow,** a fat homosexual.

**Spooning,** adolescent exploration of homosexual be-havior.

**Star,** a male homosexual.

**Station,** cruising grounds for homosexuals, e.g., bus, train depot, park bench, toilets.

**Statue Queen,** young gay in love with himself.

**Straight,** a heterosexual.

**Sugar Mama,** effeminate homosexual.

**Swish,** a passive homosexual.

**Tampered,** having experienced homosexuality at an early age.

**Tea Room,** public rest rooms used for cruising.

**Telephone Hustlers,** those who leave their phone num-bers on walls of public toilets.

**Tender Chick,** homosexually unexperienced teenage girl.

**Tent,** homosexual's room.

**Third Sex,** homosexuality.

**Three B's,** bars, baths, beaches.

**Tijuana Bible,** pornography.

**Toilet Queen,** homosexual cruising men's rooms for sex. (Also referred to as washroom faggots).

**Tondalayo,** easily recognized homosexual.

**Toss Freaks,** homosexual lovers who take turns being passive and active.

**Transvestite,** a man who receives satisfaction from dressing in women's clothing.

**Triss,** effeminate.

**Troll,** a gay cruising around toilets.

**Twinkie,** an attractive homosexual boy.

**Vamp,** an old homosexual.

**Vampire,** old homosexual who swoops down on young boys. (see Chicken Hawk)

**Van Dyke,** lesbian with traces of a moustache.

**Voyeurism,** the practice of obtaining sexual gratification by viewing sexual objects, e.g., peeping Tom.

**Vultures,** old queens posing the threat of competition to other homosexuals.

**Wall Queen,** homosexual who reads bathroom walls.

**Whore,** trashy homosexual.

**Widowed Aunt,** well-to-do homosexual who survives his late lover.

**Wife,** submissive homosexual.

**Wise,** a heterosexual who understands and tolerates homosexuals.

1. Enrique T. Rueda, *The Homosexual Network,* p. 70.

Appendices

*"Prove all things; hold fast that which is good."*

— *Paul, I Thess. 5:21.*

# Appendix 1

LOS ANGELES (AP)—Gay community leaders complained today about the arrest of 40 persons in what police called a sado-masochistic slave market.

"The police department is trying to portray this as a sick, seamy event, when in fact it was just a fund-raiser," said Robert Sirico, executive director of the Los Angeles Gay Community Center. Part of the money raised, he said, was to be used for the center's venereal disease treatment clinic.

Sixty-five police department undercover agents infiltrated what they called a male slave auction Saturday night at the Mark IV Health Club and arrested 40 persons under a rarely applied slavery statute, a vice squad spokesman said. Two others were arrested on outstanding traffic warrants.

Capt. Jack Wilson said the building in which the auction took place was equipped with "dungeons and cell blocks. In the dungeons were all forms of chains and articles of restraint..."

*Associated Press*
April 14, 1976

# Appendix 2

LOS ANGELES—Sexual abuse and exploitation of an estimated 30,000 children in the Los Angeles area—predominantly boys ages 6 to 17—has spurred a crackdown by juvenile officers of the Los Angeles Police Department.

Capt. William J. Riddle, commander of the Juvenile Division, said a six-week investigation revealed that thousands of youthful victims are being subjected to "every conceivable sex crime, including acts of sado-masochism."

The figures are based on street estimates, Riddle said, and information from victims, witnesses and suspected sex offenders show that virtually all geographic areas and segments of Los Angeles society are affected by the problem.

**BASED ON THE PRELIMINARY** investigation by the police, it is estimated that:

—More than 3,000 children under the age of 14 are being exploited sexually in the Los Angeles area.

—At least 2,000 local adult males actively pursue boys under the age of 14.

—More than 25,000 juveniles from 14 to 17 years of age are used sexually by approximately 15,000 adult males.

—Pornographic materials are shown to juveniles to stimulate them sexually, and narcotics are used to lower their inhibitions.

*Los Angeles Times*
November 26, 1976

## Appendix 3

NEW ORLEANS (UPI)—A homosexual ring operating from a Boy Scout troop may have victimized hundreds of boys and "traded them like cards" to older men, police said.

"It was more or less like you trade cards or whatever type of hobby you have—stamps, whatever," said Det. Frank Weicks. He and another juvenile officer arrested three men Friday and issued warrants for three others on charges ranging from the homosexual rape of an 11-year-old boy to crimes against nature in the alleged sex ring.

The three men arrested included a Boy Scout troopmaster, his roommate and an assistant troop leader.

Officers said they confiscated magazines, printed forms and letters mailed from across the country seeking young boys for sexual favors.

Police said they discovered filing cabinets with letters dating back to 1956 from homosexuals around the country asking for young boys.

*United Press International*
September 12, 1976

## Appendix 4

"They call themselves 'chicken hawks' and they openly advertise in magazines for 'chickens.'" said Coral Gables Police Sgt. Tony Raimondo. "The 'hawks' are grown men…homosexuals. The chickens are boys, ages 10 to 14. The 'hawks' want the 'chickens' for sex. The 'hawks' take pictures of themselves with the 'chickens' and pass them around. It is a disgusting business."

Raimondo said that in the course of an investigation which started last summer, he traced "hawks" and their "chickens" from Miami to New Orleans and back.

One "hawk," said Raimondo, was principal of a private school. He has since resigned and the school has changed hands. Raimondo said he knows of three homosexuals who managed to get certificates to operate foster homes for boys in Florida. "They go after the boys in trouble, or the ones whose parents don't care," says Raimondo.

Raimondo, who heads the Gables Youth Resources Unit, says he and his partner, Steve Spooner, have turned the results of their investigation over to State Attorney Richard Gerstein. "I think we have enough to charge a number of people," said Raimondo. "But I'm a policeman and not an attorney."

*Miami News*
March 30, 1977

## Appendix 5

Despite the campaign to clean up the area and despite police surveillance of the operation, the Playland amusement arcade on West 42nd St. near Seventh Ave. has for months been the location of a bustling, takeout boy market.

"The penny arcade is still thriving because all the police can see are kids talking to adults and then walking away," said Sgt. William McCarthy, a prostitution expert of the police Public Morals Division. "And that's not a crime."

The going price for the sex services of a Playland "chicken" (as boy prostitutes are called) is $15, and the business follows a regular pattern:

"Some of the boys you see are only 8," says a lanky 15-year-old Brooklyn boy who is a veteran of the arcade. "No one forces anyone. They hustle for money, not for sex. It's one way a kid can make a couple of hundred dollars a week."

Police complain that because of budget cuts they don't have the manpower to adequately patrol the pickup trade. And because many cautious customers take their "chicken" home, McCarthy said, there is the added task of obtaining a search warrant quickly enough to enter while the action is in progress.

*New York Daily News*
April 9, 1976

# Appendix 6

BOSTON (AP)—Fifteen men—including a mechanic, a psychiatrist and a former assistant headmaster of an exclusive boy's school—were arrested Thursday in what authorities called a ring where homosexuals from around the nation staged sordid parties with boys as young as 9.

"This is a bunch of guys who liked to get together and party with little boys," said Assistant Suffolk County District Attorney Thomas E. Peisch. "This is sex for hire . . . People patronizing it came from all over the country."

He said the ring, operating out of a home in Revere, just north of Boston, came to the attention of police earlier this year when a school bus driver was convicted of raping young boys. In the ensuing investigation, 17 men were labeled as members of the ring and seven others were named as engaging in child sex in incidents not directly tied to the ring.

With secret indictments, police on Thursday started a series of dawn arrests, rounding up suspects here, in New York and Georgia. Men were sought in five other states.

The suspects, handcuffed together and some wearing business suits, covered their faces as they piled out of police wagons to be booked on charges that officials said went back over several years that the sex ring was operating.

*Associated Press*
December 9, 1977

# Appendix 7

NEW YORK—The Episcopal bishop of New York says that many clergymen in his Church have been homosexuals, and that the ordination of an avowed lesbian as a deacon in the Church is a sign of a healthy change.

The Right Rev. Paul Moore, Jr., commenting this week on the ordination last week of Ellen Barrett, said, "Historically many of the finest clergy in our church have had this personality structure, but only recently has the social climate made it possible to be open about it."

He noted that Deacon Barrett has spoken openly about her homosexuality and, "I believe that this openness is a healthy development in our culture and our Church." He said he believed the deacon's frankness showed "courage and compassion in her identification with the gay community" and was "a credit to her."

188

The bishop observed that "homosexuality is a condition which one does not choose; it is not a question of morality."

Deacon Barrett has been studying at the General Theological Seminary in New York City. She is a contributing editor to "Integrity: Gay Episcopal Forum," the newsletter of national organization of homosexual Episcopalians.

*Associated Press*
December 27, 1975

## Appendix 8

**States of Desire: Travels in Gay America.** *By Edmund White. 336 pages. Dutton. $12.95.*

San Francisco is the S&M capital of the country, Edmund White tells us as he ticks off the baths and leather bars in its warehouse district: "At the Black and Blue the customers are so butch they swill Perrier water right out of the bottle (the bartenders jam the lime down into it)."

Fear of transvestism is fear of homosexuality, and until we accept drag queens we have not accepted ourselves. He observes that the feminist movement was astute in deciding to endorse radical lesbianism—recognizing that the hostile labeling of liberated women as "dykes" was a test case of chauvinist antagonism. "In the same way, gay men would be well advised to recognize that antipathy toward drag queens is in reality an aversion to us all...Gay unanimity is the only strong policy advisable."

This is strong medicine. White offers a still more unpalatable dose when he describes a sympathetic interview he conducted with a 36-year-old Boston man who met his 12-year-old lover when the boy was 9. Pedophilia is the touchiest of the homosexual issues, and few will be able to read this chapter without queasiness.

*Newsweek*
February, 1980

## Appendix 9

Declaring that the day is coming when there no longer be a stigma attached to homosexuality, 65 people from all over the country have organized the National Association of Gay and Lesbian Democratic Clubs.

Fourteen members of the group, which men yesterday at a Center City hotel, are delegates to the 1982 Democratic National Party Conference being held here. The group's goals are to increase the party's awareness of issues affecting homosexuals and to encourage passage of legislation to end discrimination against homosexuals in housing, employment and other areas.

Despite the successes of candidates who have had the active support of gay voters in several cities in the last two years, those who met yesterday confessed a lack of national unity. They said, too, that they had been unsuccessful in persuading the Reagan administration to oppose discrimination against homosexuals.

"Increasingly, we've made the difference (in several local elections), and we're going to network this more effectively, we hope, so that the strength we developed at the local level can have more of a voice and focus in national Democratic politics," said group chairman Tom Chorlton, who is president of the Gertrude Stein Democratic Club, a gay group in Washington.

The organizers, most of them men, held workshops in the Raphael Room of the Holiday Inn Center City on the subjects of increasing communications among the more than 85 gay political groups in the United States and of establishing new clubs.

They plan to endorse and raise funds for national candidates and to establish a national headquarters for lobbying and organizing in Washington. The first year's budget has been set at $35,000.

Chorlton said most politically active homosexuals in the United States tend to be Democrats because of the party's traditional role as an advocate of the rights of minority groups.

The newly organized association pledged also to press for equal rights for women and blacks and other minorities.

The organizers gave a standing ovation to Sen. Alan Cranston (D., Calif.), co-sponsor of the National Gay Rights Bill, which is currently stymied in Congress.

In a brief but enthusiastic speech, Cranston cited the successes of gay political activists who had helped elect candidates they supported in recent state and local elections.

Cranston said homosexuals were victims of "false stereotypes" and predicted an end to discrimination.

"Victory won't come easy, but come it will, I am convinced," he said.

John Hilferty
*Philadelphia Inquirer*
June 25, 1982

# Appendix 10

WHEN THE DEMOCRATIC National Committee voted to accept lesbians and gay men as an official party caucus. DNC political director Ann Lewis said the significance was that there were no "fireworks" among Democrats.

Indeed, there was remarkably little attention paid to the development from any quarter. Instead it seems to have been simply the latest installment in the increasingly familiar story of growing gay political influence and acceptance.

That impression is strengthened by the treatment the gay rights issue is getting from Democratic presidential hopefuls. Sen. Alan Cranston already has become a sponsor of the Senate gay civil rights bill. Gary Hart is expected to follow suit before taking to the podium as keynote speaker at a Los Angeles gay fund raising dinner April 23. Former Vice President Walter Mondale served as keynoter at another gay fund-raiser last fall.

John Glenn abandoned his earlier reticence on the issue to tell New York magazine that he favors civil rights protection for gays. Even Reuben Askew, who once publicly backed Anita Bryant's campaign to deny civil rights protection to gays, now says he is rethinking the issue in terms of "social justice," although he is not yet ready to consider it a "civil rights" issue.

By Larry Bush
*The Washington Post*
March 13, 1983

# Appendix 11

Not so long ago homosexuals in government were hounded almost as fiercely as communists. But in recent years the stigma has faded in most federal agencies. The chief exception is the CIA, and now the agency's antihomosexual policy has come under legal attack.

Last January "John Doe," a nine-year CIA veteran assigned to an undercover job, told a security officer that he had been engaging in homosexual acts for about six years. An investigation followed, and "Doe" was fired in May. In July he filed suit, seeking reinstatement and back pay. The case may not be decided for several months.

The CIA has no blanket ban on gays, according to agency spokesman Dale Peterson, but it does examine carefully the possiblity that a security-cleared employee's sexual conduct might expose him to blackmail or reflect on his mental stability. In his complaint, "Doe" argues that because he has told both family and friends of his homosexuality, he is not vulnerable to coercion. He also says that a CIA lie-detector test showed he had never divulged classified information to an unauthorized person, nor engaged in sexual acts with any foreign national. Besides, he says, the CIA does not fire heterosexual employees who engage in extramarital relationships that could make them targets for blackmail.

Since 1975, when new Civil Service rules forebade discrimination in most federal departments, even the exempted security agencies have softened their stands. According to Washington gay activist Franklin Kameny, the Defense Department "almost routinely" grants clearances to gay civilian employees. But the CIA, Kameny says, is still an "adamant offender." He warns of more legal battles to come.

*Newsweek*
September 20, 1982

# Appendix 12

In an unprecedented action, the United Church of Christ has prepared for its local congregations a study guide that anticipates the ordination of homosexuals to the church's ministry.

"It would seem," the guide says, "that a gay or lesbian person would be subject to the same understanding, procedures and criteria for ordination as would any candidate for the ministry."

"However," it adds, "the subject of homosexuality is complex and currently quite controversial.

"There are many different, and often conflicting, viewpoints about homosexuality," it says. "Likewise, there are many different, and often conflicting, viewpoints about the ordination of a gay or lesbian person."

No issue has convulsed U.S. church life more in recent years than the ordination of homosexuals. Most denominations still insist that homosexuality is a sin and the overwhelming number of religious bodies forbid ordination of avowed, practicing homosexuals to their ministry.

Although a number of pastors and priests have acknowledged their homosexuality in recent years, nearly all of those professions have occurred after ordination rather than before.

In the 1.8 million-member United Church of Christ, its 6,491 local churches are independent of all outside control and ordination to the ministry is usually carried out by an association of churches, acting at the request of the local congregation of which the person to be ordained is a minister.

The national denomination has no say about who shall or shall not be ordained but does provide standards that are usually respected by the associations.

Prepared by the denomination's Office for Church Life and Leadership, the study guide was created to aid local church decision-makers in finding their way through the mass or contradictory opinion on the issue.

It notes first that the national church's "Manual on the Ministry," which contains ministerial standards, does not take up the matter of professional homosexuals.

The guide says it hopes such a study, taking local ministry committee members through a step-by-step process of looking at the issue, "will prepare a committee for a responsible and faithful consideration for the ordination of a gay or lesbian person, if or when such a request is made."

Organized around five study sessions for members of local ministry committee, the study offers biblical, medical-psychological and legal-ethical perspectives with suggestions for further reading, study and discussion.

One session also calls for identifying local ministry committee members' identifying assumptions on the issue of homosexuality, including a short questionnaire aimed at eliciting members' knowledge and attitudes toward the issue.

By David E. Anderson
UPI Religion Writer
October 25, 1980

## Appendix 13

A dark and sometimes desperate segment of Tulsa's homosexual community concentrates on downtown streets.

It's the lower end of the city's subculture spectrum. It writhes. It thrives. And, Tulsa police say, it grows.

Central in the nighttime is the rectangle formed by Main Street and Boulder Avenue and Sixth and Ninth streets.

Police officers and street people call it "The Fruit Loop."

Homosexual favors—bodies—are for only slightly surreptitious sale.

Police arrest a half dozen or more offenders for solicitation each week, vice squad Lt. Drew Diamond says.

The Fruit Loop's atmosphere and aura are shabby, sordid, sullen, spiteful, false—and too real—police say.

Hope and tolerance also surface, but those qualities are almost always tinged with a sad spoken sense of defiance, loss and loneliness that prevails from deep dusk until dawn, an observer finds.

Transvestites dot homosexual haunts near the Fruit Loop. (They are not necessarily homosexual).

Runaways and other young men exploring and/or entering homosexuality wait on its curbs, walk its perimeters nightly.

"Hustlers" work it. They offer—and supply, for as little as $10— homosexual sex acts to suport themselves for a time on the streets and on the Main Mall.

"Most of these people that come out here won't pay more than $20," an outspoken 24-year-old male prostitue said as he sat on the front steps of Holy Family Cathedral at 11 p.m.

"Sometimes. I get $30 or $40. I've had then approach me for $10. I won't take it. Hey $20 is bad enough, really ridiculous, but $10 is just super-ridiculous."

"It's the bottom, the real pits," one 19-year-old 'amateur' homosexual said while he waited and hoped the same night for a pick-up in the 800 block of South Main Street.

"But it's all I got, and a lover's all I want right now."

His stepfather forced him into sodomy when he "was 12 or 13," he said, "and well, hell, yes, I got to like it."

*Tulsa World*
Sunday, July 11, 1982

## Appendix 14

WASHINGTON (AP)—American homosexual leaders emerged from an unprecedented meeting at the White House on Saturday, declaring talks with a Carter administration official demonstrated the President's commitment to human rights extends to gay people.

In a three-hour session, Margaret Constanza, Carter's assistant for public liaison, heard grievances aired against the government on several fronts by 10 members of the National Gay Task Force. She had agreed to the meeting a month earlier.

The meeting, which took place while President Jimmy Carter and his family were spending the weekend at Camp David, Md., was described by one participant as "a happy milestone on the road to full equality under the law for gay men and women."

THE PARTICIPANTS SAID THEY were assured that Carter was aware of the meeting, and they noted that during his presidential campaign he promised to support legislation aimed at eliminating hiring discrimination within the government on the basis of sexual preferences.

In addition to military and immigration grievances, the group seeks stronger measures to insure the safety of gay prisoners, tax deductible status for gay organizations, and federal grants for research and social services on gay issues.

*Associated Press*
March 27, 1977

## Appendix 15

HOUSTON (AP)—Gay ministers gathering here for their 10th convention between Christianity and homosexuality.

But, among other issues on the six-day agenda of the Universal Fellowship of Metropolitan Community Churches, the ministers are trying to resolve a delicate semantic issue they have inherited from trational Christianity: how to refer to the deity.

A task force assigned to the issue has recommended a change toward more "inclusive" language than such enduring references as "Lord and Master." Instead, the 3,000 delegates will consider more "sexually balanced" terms such as "Nurturer" and even "the Breasted One."

Dr. Richard J. Follett of Hollywood, Calif., the church's media representative, conceded Tuesday the Old Testament book of Leviticus forbids sex between two men, "But it also said don't eat shrimp, don't eat lobster and women should not wear red.

"The only people who use that argument that I can respect are Orthodox Jewish rabbis," said Follett, noting Orthodox Jews observe the strictures of Leviticus.

The church, organized in 1968 to accept practicing homosexuals, claims more than 25,000 members in 170 congregations, including women and some homosexuals. Some members also belong to other denominations. All members are considered "ministers," according to Follett, who is also executive director of the Samaritan Theological Institute in Hollywood.

Founder Troy Perry, 43, established the church 13 years ago after being excommunicated from the fundamentalist Church of God.

Perry, an evangelical preacher at age 15 is his hometown of Tallahassee, Fla., and the father of two sons from a heterosexual marriage, said at a news conference Tuesday his church believes its members should be ruled by conscience.

"We're very concerned with not whether people are married or not, but rather with the commitment," Perry said. He said his sect requires only "mental monogamy" of its members that he doesn't believe love for one person necessarily precludes love for another.

*Associated Press*
*August 6, 1981*

## Appendix 16

RIVERSIDE, Calif. (AP)—A teen-age boy said he was "glad I have a father now" after social service officials approved his adoption by his foster father, a 29-year-old homosexual man.

An attempt by David Frater to adopt Kevin Frater, a heterosexual high school student, won endorsement by the Riverside County Department of Public Social Services on Thursday.

Although a judge makes the final determination on adoptions, the social services department usually makes a recommendation to the court, said Gloria Allred, attorney for David Frater.

No court date has been set for final approval, Ms. Allred said, but "we forsee no difficulty now that they (county officials) have recommended the adoption."

Kevin Frater, 17, has lived with his foster father for two years.

"I'm really happy," Kevin said Thursday. "I knew that we were going to win all along."

The social services department previously had refused to endorse or oppose the adoption "because it was afraid of setting the precedent of allowing an openly homosexual person to adopt a child," Ms. Allred said. "They engaged in a course of delay, footdragging and stonewalling to prevent the adoption."

"It's our belief that homosexuals should have the same right to adopt as heterosexual adults do," Ms. Allred said. "There are thousands of children who are waiting for adoption, and it's unfair to deny these children the right to a caring and nurturing parental relationship solely because of *the adopting adult's sexual preference*."

*December 10, 198*

# Appendix 17

98TH CONGRESS
1ST SESSION

# S. 430

To prohibit employment discrimination on the basis of sexual orientation.

---

## IN THE SENATE OF THE UNITED STATES

FEBURARY 3 (legislative day, JANUARY 25), 1983

Mr. TSONGAS (for himself, Mr. CRANSTON, Mr. PACKWOOD, Mr. MOYNIHAN, and Mr. KENNEDY) introduced the following bill; which was read twice and referred to the Committee on Labor and Human Resources

---

# A BILL

To prohibit employment discrimination on the basis of sexual orientation.

1     *Be it enacted by the Senate and House of Representa-*
2 *tives of the United States of America in Congress assembled,*

3         EQUAL EMPLOYMENT OPPORTUNITIES

4     SECTION 1. (a) Sections 703(a), 703(b), 703(c), 703(d),
5 703(e), 703(j), 704(b), 706(g), and 717(a) of the Civil Rights
6 Act of 1964 (42 U.S.C. 2000e–2 (a), (b), (c), (d), (e), and
7 (j), –3(b), –5(g), and –16(a)) are amended by inserting after
8 "sex" each place it appears a comma and the following:
9 "sexual orientation".

## Appendix 18

98TH CONGRESS
1ST SESSION

# H. R. 2624

To prohibit discrimination on the basis of affectional or sexual orientation, and for
other purposes.

---

## IN THE HOUSE OF REPRESENTATIVES

### APRIL 19, 1983

Mr. WEISS (for himself, Mr. WAXMAN, Mr. LOWRY of Washington, Mr. AUCOIN,
Mr. STUDDS, Mr. YATES, Mr. TORRICELLI, Mr. FRANK, Mr. TOWNS, Mr.
SOLARZ, Mr. FAUNTROY, Mr. DELLUMS, Mr. CLAY, Mr. MILLER of Califor-
nia, Mrs. BOXER, Mr. SUNIA, Mrs. SCHROEDER, Mr. DIXON, Mr. WEAVER,
Mr. GARCIA, Mr. FAZIO, Mr. MORRISON of Connecticut, Mr. EDWARDS of
California, Mr. BERMAN, Mr. BATES, Mr. McKINNEY, Mr. CROCKETT, Mr.
MITCHELL, Mr. EDGAR, Mr. GREEN, Mr. LEVINE of California, Mr.
ROYBAL, Mr. RANGEL, Mr. KOSTMAYER, Mr. SABO, Mr. STARK, Mr. DY-
MALLY, Mrs. COLLINS, Mr. BONIOR of Michigan, Mr. FOGLIETTA, Mr. SI-
KORSKI, Mr. WHEAT, Mr. LEHMAN of Florida, Mr. STOKES, Mr. SHANNON,
Mr. BARNES, Mr. HOWARD, Mr. LELAND, Ms. MIKULSKI, Mr. CONYERS,
Mr. BORSKI, Mr. RICHARDSON, Mr. MATSUI, Mr. PANETTA, Mr. DICKS,
Mr. COYNE, Mr. HOYER, Mr. SCHUMER, and Mr. GRAY) introduced the fol-
lowing bill; which was referred jointly to the Committees on Education and
Labor and the Judiciary

---

# A BILL

To prohibit discrimination on the basis of affectional or sexual
orientation, and for other purposes.

1   *Be it enacted by the Senate and House of Representa-*

2   *tives of the United States of America in Congress assembled,*

3   That this Act may be cited as the "Civil Rights Amendments

4   Act of 1983".

# Appendix 19

98TH CONGRESS
1ST SESSION

# H. R. 427

To prohibit discrimination on the basis of affectional or sexual orientation, and for other purposes.

---

## IN THE HOUSE OF REPRESENTATIVES

JANUARY 3, 1983

Mr. WEISS (for himself, Mr. BURTON of California, Mr. WAXMAN, and Mr. LOWRY of Washington) introduced the following bill; which was referred jointly to the Committees on the Judiciary and Education and Labor

---

# A BILL

To prohibit discrimination on the basis of affectional or sexual orientation, and for other purposes.

1    *Be it enacted by the Senate and House of Representa-*
2 *tives of the United States of America in Congress assembled,*
3 That this Act may be cited as the "Civil Rights Amendments
4 Act of 1983"

5                PUBLIC FACILITIES

6    SEC. 2. Section 301(a) of the Civil Rights Act of 1964
7 (42 U.S.C. 2000b(a)) is amended by inserting after "reli-
8 gion," the following: "affectional or sexual orientation,".

**DEMOCRATIC**
NATIONAL COMMITTEE   1625 Massachusetts Ave., N.W.   Washington, D.C. 20036   (202) 797-5900

Charles T. Manatt
Chairman

August 30, 1982

Mr. Tom Chorlton
National Association of Gay and Lesbian Democratic Clubs
1742 Massachusetts Avenue, S.E.
Washington, D.C.  20003

Dear Tom,

Thank you for updating me on the progress of the National
Association of Gay and Lesbian Democratic Clubs.

As I said in speaking to your first conference in Philadelphia on June 24th, I consider formation of the national
association an important step toward our common goal: a
strong Democratic Party working to achieve full human rights
and civil rights for every American.

Toward this end, I know that you share my pride that the
statements adopted by the National Party Conference reflected
the commitment of this party to end any discrimination based
on sexual orientation.  Let us work to ensure that the unan-
imous action of the NPC, which has been widely praised as
reflecting a united Democratic Party, is an indication of
further gains to be made.

Ann Lewis tells me that she is working with you on a
positive, campaign-oriented program of assistance to Democratic
candidates in our critical elections this year.  Please continue to keep me informed.

Cordially,

Charles T. Manatt
Chairman

CTM:alb

COPY FOR INTERNAL USE ONLY

# Appendix 21

No state in the union officially recognizes gay marriages. But homosexuals continue to push hard for the same legal rights that society accords married couples. "The old Donna Reed version of the family is no longer what most Americans experience," says Harry Britt, the only avowedly gay member of the board of supervisors of San Francisco, a city where single adults outnumber the married, and homosexuals make up 15% to 20% of the population. In response to those demographic facts of life, Britt last week persuaded his fellow supervisors to pass a startling measure that would allow the city's employees to sign up their lovers for spouselike health benefits. The ordinance is the first of its kind in the country.

The measure applies to unmarried heterosexual couples as well as homosexual partners over 18, but there is little question that the idea was gay-inspired. To qualify for the benefits, couples unrelated by blood or marriage pay a $23 filing fee, then swear that they "share the common necessities of life." If the relationship breaks up, a person must inform the city and wait six months before claiming a new partner. Mayor Dianne Feinstein has not yet signed the legislation, but since it passed by an 8 to 3 vote, her veto would probably be overridden.

The new rules require the city to treat all qualifying live-in partners as if they were spouses. For instance, they will have the same visitation rights at local jails and hospitals, and city workers would get a day off to attend a mate's funeral. But what backers were most eager to win was low cost ($50 a month) health benefits, which city employees will pay for at the same rate as they do for a husband or wife.

*Time*
December 13, 1982

# Appendix 22

*So God created man in his own image; in the image of God created he him; male and female created he them ... And God said unto them, Be fruitful, and multiply ...*

—Genesis 1:27-28

To many readers of the Bible this passage is scriptural proof that heterosexual union is God's own design for human nature. But in every generation God has also created a percentage of men and women who are powerfully drawn to members of the same sex. For those homosexuals who are also Christians or Jews, there ususally have been only two choices: either repress their own sexuality or renounce their faith. Increasingly, however, religious homosexuals are adopting a third and more positive approach. They are insisting that since God made them the way they are, they have every right to share with heterosexuals in the life of church and synagogue. In their new and often militant mood, gays are challenging religious establishments to support the gay-rights movement and rethink traditional sexual morality.

The pressure is greatest in San Francisco, where an estimated 20 percent of the population is homosexual. Last month that city's Roman Catholic archdiocese received an explosive report on gay and lesbian issues from a task force of its Commission on Social Justice. Citing recent violence against homosexuals, the panel, which included both straights and gays, charged the archdiocese and its leader, Archbishop John R. Quinn, with tacitly encouraging antihomosexual attitudes. More important, the report demanded that the church welcomed gay men into the priesthood, upgrade services to the gay community and acknowledge the unique spiritual experience of devout homosexual Catholics. The archdiocese noncommittally accepted the report as a "working document"—a first step, gay Catholic activists believe, toward bringing a whole range of highly volatile issues out of the church's closet.

*Newsweek*
October 11, 1982

# Appendix 23

The promiscuous homosexual male has long been vulnerable to hepatitis and venereal diseases like syphilis and gonorrhea. But an unusual assortment of disorders—some of them deadly—have broken out in the homosexual community. Among them: intestinal infections usually seen in the tropics, a particularly virulent form of pneumonia and a lethal cancer most often found in equatorial Africa. "The health problems of homosexuals used to be no different from those of heterosexuals," says New York internist Dr. Ronald J. Grossman. "But in the last five or six years there's been a major change."

The epidemic does not affect homosexual women: it seems closely linked to the life-style of gay men with many sexual contacts. It coincides with the burgeoning of bathhouses, gay bars, and bookstores in major cities where homosexual men meet. "The large numbers of anonymous contacts in gay bathhouses increases the risk of sexually transmitted diseases exponentially," says Dr. Daniel C. William, a New York physician with a large homosexual practice. According to the Centers for Disease Control nearly 50 percent of males with active syphilis are homosexual. Hepatitis B is so prevalent among homosexual men that blood serum from gay volunteers was used in the development of the new vaccine against the disease.

Dramatic Spread: Male homosexuals are particularly prone to intestinal disorders if they combine oral and anal sex practices. In San Francisco the number of cases of amebiasis has risen 7,000 percent since 1974, and shigellosis and giardiasis have also spread with dramatic swiftness. "No modern city should have this many cases," says Dr. Selma Dritz of the city's Bureay of Disease Control and Adult Health. "The problem is person-to-person transmission."

Newsweek<br>
December 21, 1981

## Appendix 24

Jack is one of 913 people across the U.S. battling against the deadly new syndrome known as AIDS (Acquired Immune Defiency Syndrome); 228 others have already succumbed. First fully described in 1980, the disease destroys the immune system, leaving its victims prey to all manner of viruses and bacteria. Cancer, particularly KS, is a major threat, as is *pneumocystis carinii* pneumonia, a singularly lethal ailment. The survival rate after two years of AIDS: less than 20%. Last week, at New York University Medical Center in Manhattan, 300 doctors gathered to exchange notes on the phenomenon. The bad news: "We are at the horizon of a new epidemic, rather than at the peak," says Dr. James Curran, director of the AIDS task force at the Centers for Disease Control (CDC) in Atlanta. Half the known cases of AIDS have been diagnosed in the past six months, and the number of new cases has been doubling every eight to twelve months. Says Curran: "We are no longer acting like a quick solution is just around the corner. This epidemic will be with us the rest of our lives."

The big question in AIDS is who will be affected next. So far, the disease has mostly stricken homosexual men (72% of all cases), intravenous drug abusers (17%), Haitian immigrants (4%) and hemophiliacs (1%). But a majority of the experts believe that what was once known as the "gay plague" will enter the general population. Because of their frequent contact with AIDS patients and blood, "hospital workers will be next," predicts Dr. Roger Enlow, a leading AIDS researcher. As head of New York City's brand-new office of gay and lesbian health concerns, Enlow monitors new cases of AIDS and refers them to various support groups.

*Time*
March 28, 1983

## Appendix 25

SAN FRANCISCO (AP)—The incurable disease known as AIDS has afflicted one in every 350 unmarried men in three heavily homosexual neighborhoods, according to a draft of a study reported Wednesday by the San Francisco Chronicle.

And the authors of the report, being prepared for publication in the British medical journal Lancet, say their figures probably underestimated the rate of Acquired Immune Deficiency Syndrome among homosexual males.

The mysterious disease, which leaves the body susceptible to a number of deadly infections, has been diagnosed in 204 San Francisco Bay area men since 1980 and 53 have died, said Dr. Selma Dritz, chief of San Francisco's bureau of communicable disease control.

She said she expects 250 to 300 new cases of the disease to be detected in San Francisco this year.

AIDS "will inevitably become epidemic throughout the nation," said Dr. James W. Curran, who heads the AIDS task force at the federal Centers for Disease Control in Atlanta.

Already, 1,200 cases have been reported since the disease was recognized three years ago and the federal centers expect 1,500 new cases this year. Only 14 percent of patients have survived three years after their diagnosis.

The study was conducted by two researchers at the University of California in San Francisco, Dr. Michale Gorman, an epidemiologist, and Dr. Andrew Moss, a biomedical statistician.

They studied the incidence of AIDS among never-married men over the age of 15 in the heavily gay neighborhoods of the Castro, Noe Valley and Haight districts.

The incidence they discovered was "extremely high," said Dr. Richard Selik of the CDC.

March 24, 1983

# Appendix 26

A new and deadly disease is coursing through the country, wasting the bodies of victims, incubating in an untold number of others who have yet to show the symptoms and triggering one of the most intensive investigations of an epidemic in medical history.

Since it came into public view in 1981, derisively called "The Gay Plague," AIDS (Acquired Immune Deficiency Syndrome), which ravages the body's immune system, has stricken 1,300 Americans— more than half of them in the last year. And there is no cure in sight. "In my professional career, I have never encountered a more frustrating and depressing situation," says Dr. Peter Mansell of Houston's M.D. Anderson Hospital and Tumor Institute. "People who you know are likely to die ask what they can do to help themselves, and you are forced to say, more or less, 'I have no idea'."

The death toll to date—489—is far higher than the combined fatalities from Legionnaire's disease and toxic shock syndrome. Fewer than 14 percent of AIDS victims have survived more than three years after being diagnosed, and no victim has recovered fully. The lethal disease, first reported in the homosexual communities of New York, Los Angeles and San Francisco, has spread to 35 states and 16 foreign countries, including France, Germany and Denmark. And although gay men still account for 72 percent of cases, AIDS seems to be moving into the population at large. First, intravenous drug users of both sexes, then Haitian immigrants, and more recently, the sex partners and children of both groups have been afflicted. Hemophiliacs and at least one recipient of a routine blood transfusion have also been stricken. And then there are those who fall into no apparent category.

"As the months go by, we see more and more groups," says Dr. Anthony Fauci of the National Institute of Allergy and Infectious Diseases. "AIDS is creeping out of well-defined epidemiological confines." According to Dr. Jeffrey Koplan, a public health expert at the U.S. Centers for Disease Control in Atlanta, Ga., AIDS will begin appearing with greater frequency among heterosexuals as the epidemic grows. And growth is one thing most AID researchers seem sure of: by the end of this year, predicts Dr. James Curran, head of CDC's AIDS Task Force, there will be more than 2,000 cases. "It has caught everybody by surprise," says Dr. Abe Macher of the National Institues of Health. "Textbooks are being rewritten. We're observing the evolution of a new disease."

*Newsweek*
*April 18, 1983*

# Appendix 27

The four young men sat in the semi-darkness of the deserted ward waiting for their weekend shot of interferon at New York's Memorial Sloan-Kettering Cancer Center. They tried not to look at the fifth man, the law professor. His face was swollen and disfigured by purplish Kaposi's sarcoma (KS) lesions; his frail body, wracked for months by pneumonia and other recurring infections, weighed no more than a child's. He was beyond hope, beyond terror. They fought not to see their fate in his. And again they fought the old fears and doubts. Their life-style was not sinful. AIDS was not a gay plague sent down upon them. "God doesn't do things like this," said Alan, a quiet Southerner who works in a bank and sings in church choirs. "I'm not being punished for anything. It's bad luck or fate or something I have done that has caused this to happen."

The nightmare rumors that swirled through the homosexual communities of New York, San Francisco and Los Angeles almost three years ago have become cruel fact. The dire warnings in the gay press were well-founded. Suddenly, everyone seems to know an AIDS victim. The disease's drawn-out incubation period has thousands of gay men sweating in terror, seeing every bruise as a Kaposi's sarcoma lesion; every cough, the onset of *Pneumocystis carinii* pneumonia. AIDS is not a gay plague. If it had not developed first among homosexuals, it could well have struck some other risk group. But clearly, urban gay life-style has put many homosexual males at risk. An infectious agent loose in the hothouse environment of a gay bath, where some men have as many as 10 anonymous sexual contacts in one night, would spread exponentially. Ironically, the freedom, the promiscuity, the hypermasculinity that many gays declared an integral part of their culture have come to haunt them. "Isn't it something that what brought most of here now leaves tens of thousands of us wondering whether that celebration ends in death?" says Randy Shilts, a San Francisco journalist.

"People are afraid to go out with each other. Some are abstaining." And others, instead of cruising are dating for the first time.

The hundreds of confirmed AIDS victims struggling for their lives no longer have such choices. Discriminated against by insurance companies wary of the staggering medical costs of the disease, often shunned by nervous co-workers and avoided by former lovers, the least fortunate have become untouchables—alone, helpless and despairing. Even those able to handle the emotional and financial burdens suffer cruelly. "I've felt that people were treating me like a leper," says KS patient Michael McAdory, manager of a gay night-

206

club in Houston. "I'd walk into a room and hear people say, 'That's him. He's the one who has AIDS'".

Many stricken gays have had to bear the double burden of breaking the news of their illness and their homosexuality to their families at the same time. "Many gay men who have never been reconciled to their gayness have been crippled by the knowledge they are dying of a gay-related disease," says Los Angeles physician Joel Weisman. "It's like a second coming out." As he watched victims abandoned by family and friends who could not deal with the stigma, Weisman felt compelled to speak out in their behalf.

'Russian Roulette': The shared wisdom in the gay community these days is that you "change your life-style, not your sexuality." But as Dr. Weisman points out in L.A.: "Some gays don't want to change and continue playing Russian roulette." Still, many more say tentatively that they have moved beyond shock and fear and anger to a feeling of relief that they finally have a medical reason to slow down their lives.

*Newsweek*
April 18, 1983

# Appendix 28

The Hothouse was legendary in gay San Francisco—a four-story, 10,000-square-foot pleasure palace filled with inviting private alcoves and the paraphernalia of kinky sex: harnesses, chains and shackles. Its centerpiece, boyish and innocent amid the ominous clutter of leather restraining devices, was a giant tire swing—a symbol, as owner Louis Gaspar liked to say, "of all the things you were afraid to do as a child, especially if you had any gay tendencies." That was how Gaspar saw the Hothouse—as a moneymaker, sure enough, but also as a sort of therapeutic playpen, "a place where gay men could live out their adolescence, sexually and playfully, because so many of us never got through that phase." Last month the Hothouse went out of business, a victim of the gay community's rising fears about the connection between promiscuous, anonymous sex and the AIDS epidemic. Gaspar was philosophic—the place had served its purpose, and anyway, he said, things were getting "too far out"—but his clientele was in despair. "This is depressing," said one young man, picking his way through the remnants of the Hothouse's once abundant supply of exotic sexual appliances. "Not only is *this* over—it's *all* over."

For Gay America, a decade of carefree sexual adventure, a headlong gambol on the far side of the human libido, has all but come to a close. The flag of sexual liberation that had flown as the symbol of the gay movement has been lowered. Caution and responsibility—to oneself, to one's friends, to the larger and still pressing concern of gay life in America—are now the watchwords of gay liberation, and many homosexuals do not regret it. According to the Centers for Disease Control in Atlanta, AIDS (Acquired Immune Deficiency Syndrome) has claimed 1,922 victims, more than 70 percent of whom are male homosexuals; 743 persons are dead. Though the disease seems largely confined to the four "high risk" groups (male homosexuals, intravenous drug users, Haitians and hemophiliacs), there is hardly any doubt that it is primarily communicated by homosexual male sex (page 40).

*Newsweek*
August 8, 1983

## Appendix 29

LOS ANGELES (AP)—With homosexuals taking more visible and active roles in American politics, contenders for the 1984 Democratic presidential nomination are waging unprecedented competition for their support.

Many gay and lesbian activists see the coming election year [1984] as the culmination of a decade-long evolution from a time when all except the most progressive politicians shunned ties to the gay community.

Old notions that such ties were political liabilities are being abandoned, as politicians perceive that gay support, instead of producing negative backlash, can significantly boost campaigns.

"Gays have forced their inclusion in the political process by organizing," said George Dalley, deputy campaign manager for former Vice President Walter Mondale. "They have become a political force and they have to be recognized."

Some signs of the times:

■ All eight Democratic candidates have met with gay leaders; most have spoken at gay-sponsored events.

■ All say they support federal money for research into AIDS, the immune disorder that predominantly strikes gay men.

■ Political pundits wrote off Ohio Sen. John Glenn's hopes of capturing this weekend's presidential endorsement from the National Organization for Women because he refuses to back a gay rights measure in the Senate.

■ Last month, New York Gov. Mario Cuomo, sometimes touted as future presidential material, fulfilled a 1982 campaign promise with an executive order to state agencies to halt any discrimination because of "sexual orientation."

■ For the first time, the Democratic Party, which included a gay rights plank in its 1980 platform, has a Gay Caucus in the Democratic National Committee.

In the 1980 presidential campaign, former President Jimmy Carter and Massachusetts Sen. Edward Kennedy spoke out for gay rights. But some gay activists see the 1984 campaign as a more significant signpost because of the number of candidates seeking their support, said Tom Chorlton, executive director of the National Association of Gay and Lesbian Democratic Clubs.

Mark Cohen, political director for California Sen. Alan Cranston, noting that Cranston has employed gay people on his staff for years, said, "There was a conscious effort on the part of this campaign from the beginning to work the gay vote."


The Rev. Jesse Jackson said he wants to include homosexuals and lesbians in his "rainbow coalition" of "people who have been rejected and oppressed," because gay rights is a civil rights issue.

The Mondale camp plans to develop a campaign strategy specifically targeting the gay community, said Dalley. "We know and recognize the growing political interest and power in that community and we expect to relate to it as a body that is going to be organized and ready to participate in the 1984 electoral process," he said.

Glenn created a stir last month when he announced he would not support a Senate bill to amend the Civil Rights Act and specifically ban discrimination against homosexuals. Glenn said he felt "sexual preference or lifestyle" did not fall into the category of civil rights.

He quickly added that he would not tolerate harassment of homosexuals, but the announcement received widespread publicity and criticism from gay activists.

"In the early days, many candidates did not want to take money, or they were concerned it would do them more harm than good," said Sheldon Andelson, founder and co-chairman of the Bank of Los Angeles and one of California's most prominent gay leaders. "It didn't take long to prove that it didn't hurt."

December 11, 1983

209

# Appendix 30

On March 25, 1952, Mr. Carlisle H. Humelsine, Deputy Undersecretary of State, told the House Appropriations Committee that the State Department had ousted 119 homosexuals during the previous year. Thus, almost casually, there was brought to public attention a most important and dangerous state of affairs, namely the invasion of American political life by "the men of Sodom" (Genesis 13:13).

Popular reaction to this sensational piece of news ranged all the way from righteous indignation on religious grounds to a pseudo-liberal attitude of "tolerance." However, few people bothered to inquire deeply into the facts of the matter. Even those who cautioned against homosexuals on the ground that they represented a bad security risk, did so mainly because their social vulnerability exposed them to all sorts of blackmail.

Valid as this aspect of the problem is, it is a comparatively minor one. In reality the main reason why, at this juncture of history, the elimination of the homosexuals from all Government agencies and especially the State Department is of vital urgency is that by the very nature of their vice they belong to a sinister, mysterious and efficient International.

Welded together by the identity of their forbidden desires, of their strange, sad needs, habits, dangers, not to mention their outrageously fatuous vocabulary, members of this International constitute a worldwide conspiracy against society. This conspiracy has spread all over the globe; has penetrated all classes; operated in armies and in prisons; has infiltrated into the press, the movies and the cabinets; and it all but dominates the arts, literature, theater, music and TV.

And here is why homosexual officials are a peril to us in the present struggle between West and East: members of one conspiracy are prone to join another conspiracy. This is one reason why so many homosexuals from being enemies of society in general, become enemies of capitalism in particular. Without being necessarily Marxist they serve the ends of the Communist International in the name of their rebellion against the prejudices, standards, ideals of the "bourgeois" world. Another reason for the homosexual-Communist alliance is the instability and passion for intrigue for intrigue's sake, which is inherent in the homosexual personality. A third reason is the social promiscuity within the homosexual minority and the fusion it effects between upperclass and proletarian corruption.

# Political Corruption

Sodom has always been in politics. Long before there was a Homosexual International, homosexual intrigue—sometimes on an international scale-enlivened the political and diplomatic annals. I mention only Julius Caesar's affair with King Nicomedes of Bithynia which excited his contemporaries much more than the one with Cleopatra. To paraphrase a remark of Marcel Proust—love of men led Caesar unto virility and virility unto glory, as it did some other extraordinary personalities, such as Richard Coeur de Lion and Frederick the Great of Prussia. There was the reign of the "mignons" which became the undoing of Henri II, last of the Valois Kings, and the homosexual camarilla around "Monsieur," Louis XIV's brother, which occasionally said it with murder. There is also the diplomatic agent of Louis XV, the ambiguous Chevalier d'Eton who, turning up alternately in men's and women's clothes, functioned for a while in St. Petersburg as a female reader of Elizabeth of Russia only to present himself later as an adoring *ephebe* of Frederick the Great in Potsdam.

But it was the great homosexual scandal of the early twentieth century—the Eulenberg case—which awakened public opinion to the menace of homosexuality in politics. This famous German case was first exposed in 1906 in a series of startling articles by Maximilian Harden in *Die Zukunft*. These articles charged that Prince "Phili" Eulenburg, the Kaiser's favorite, and his clique of homosexual friends, formed a "State within the State, a Government within the Government" on the very steps of the throne. "There exist," Harden claimed, "two policies, the official policy and the secret policy of Eulenburg." The latter's policy was inspired, he insisted, by the homosexual French Charge d'Affairs in Berlin and was designed to weaken the German position.

Harden could write like an avenging angel when he was angry, and he was very angry. An admirer of the late Prince Bismark, he was horrified by the rapid deterioration of the powerful Reich forged by the "Iron Chancellor," and believed he found the key to this deterioration: German public life was riddled with homosexuality. In fact, the Eulenburg scandal was preceded and paralleled by other homosexual scandals featuring high aristocrats, generals, industrialists, many of whom belonged to the Kaiser's intimate circle. Hence: Sodom delenda est! The homosexuals had to be eliminated from influential positions. No state—Harden was convinced—was strong enough to withstand their corroding influence.

I was a young child in Germany when after months of such attacks Prince Eulenburg found himself finally compelled to sue Harden for libel; I can still remember the shock it was to public opinion when Harden won. The verdict came after a long drawn-out litigation, and right up to the end the German bourgeiose was convinced that Harden was a liar. They could not believe that the scabrous stories he told about the mighty were true. Harden's final triumph spelled not only Eulenburg's but also the Kaiser's guilt. Not that Wilhelm was ever suspected of belonging to Sodom himself. However, he had shown s deplorable affinity for homosexuals and this was enough to make of the Eulenburg case the "necklace affair" of the German Empire—a morbid manifestation of a state of general depravity that later erupted into the tragedy of World War I.

With fascination I watched the little Sodoms functioning within the Embassies and foreign offices. Somehow homosexuals always seemed to come by the dozen, not because they were cheaper that way but rather because a homosexual ambassador or charge d'affaires or Undersecretary of State liked to staff his "team" with his own people. Another reason was that the homosexuals really do look after their own. "Damn it, in order to make a career one should have been abnormal." That's how Baron Holstein, Gray Eminence of the Wilhelmstrasse, commented on Harden's disclosures of this fine-meshed network of direct and indirect influences with the help of which the homosexual cliques pushed their members into important positions.

## Homosexuality and Communism

The alliance between the Homosexual International and the Communist International started at the dawn of the Pink Decade. It was then that the homosexual aristocracy—writers, poets, painters and such—discovered Marxism. Why did this bleak doctrine charm people who up to now had posed as decadent aesthetes? No doubt, the same sentiments which motivated the Communist conversion of intellectuals in general—such as opposition to Nazism and Fascism, visions of the end of capitalism and the need of a faith—played a part in the Communist conversion of homosexual intellectuals. But particular emotions gave it an additional fervor.

First of all, a sense of guilt concerning their forbidden desires and the hope to purge themselves of it by cooperating with the Worker's Movement loomed large. Then too, the Communist assumption that the workers represented the future gave a respectable face to that social promiscuity which is the secret element of their vice.

Furthermore, the promise of a classless society where everyone would be free appealed to their own need of freedom from "bourgeois" constraint. For, weren't they too an oppressed class? Weren't they too "threatened in their conditions of existence" (Communist Manifesto)? The way they figured it the Communists in fighting Capitalism were revenging them for the ostracism which capitalist society held forever dangling over their heads.

True, quite a few homosexual intellectuals soon found that Marxism wasn't all it was cracked up to be. Thus the great French writer Andre Gide—whom the European homosexuals call "our Goethe"— solemnly repudiated the god that failed. Others followed his example, especially when they discovered that Russia was by no means the homosexual paradise they had imagined.

## Natural Secret Agents

There is another even more sinister aspect of homosexuality in high places. It is that homosexuals make natural secret agents and natural traitors. This conclusion is to be drawn from a theory developed by Professor Theodor Reik in his "Psychology of Sex Relations." Briefly, this theory is that the phantasy of sex metamorphosis operating in most homosexual affairs which causes him to play the role of the other sex causes him to enjoy any job which gives him the chance of playing a double role.

The classical example is the famous espionage case of the homosexual Colonel Alfred Redl of the Austro-Hungarian Military Intelligence who, during the decade preceeding World War I, delivered Austrian military secrets to the Russians and denounced his own agents to them. He got an immense kick out of playing the role of both the traitor and of the one whose lifework it is to apprehend and punish traitors.

Traitors? On June 11, 1951, we found Member of Parliament George Wigg, in the British House of Commons debate of that day, referring to press reports of "widespread sexual perversion in the Foreign Office." This came at the time when Parliament was aroused over the mysterious affair of the two missing British diplomats who disappeared behind the Iron Curtain.

As a matter of fact, there has been in the British foreign service a long tradition of unconventional diplomats, quite a few of whom were homosexuals. In normal times this did not matter much; a homosexual diplomat would do as well by his country as a normal one, and sometimes better. But here is the point: ours are not normal times and the homosexual personality is too unstable to withstand the pressures and conflicts inherent in the struggle between East and West.

R.G. Waldeck
*Human Events*
September 29, 1960

# Appendix 31

Democratic front-runner Walter Mondale continues to make it abundantly clear: He's going all-out after the "gay" vote. The former Vice President's answers to 27 questions covering topics "important to the gay/lesbian community" were released February 9 by the National Gay Task Force (NGTF). And they reveal—on issue after issue—that Mondale lines up with the militant homosexual "rights" movement. For example:

■ Mondale promised that "If elected President, I will within the first three months of my administration issue Executive Orders banning discrimination in federal government employment on the basis of sexual orientation." These orders, he said, "would extend to federally contracted private employment."

■ Asked if he would extend the mandate of federal civil rights enforcement agencies like the U.S. Civil Rights Commission, the EEOC and the Justice Department's Civil Rights Division to include "anti-gay/lesbian bias," Mondale responded affirmatively. He said that "all government agencies dealing with civil and human rights" should fight "denial of equal opportunity based on...sexual orientation."

■ Mondale, the NGTF points out, has said that "I support in concept" extending the 1964 Civil Rights Act "to prohibit discrimination based on sexual orientation." And in the survey, while Mondale stopped short of endorsing a specific legislative approach for the moment, he made this forceful statement in favor of homosexual rights:

"I support an avenue which recognizes that discrimination against gay men and lesbians is a denial of fundamental civil rights. In matters of equal rights, there can be no double standard; either our nation is committed, as I am, to equal opportunity for all Americans, or it is not committed at all."

■ Mondale called for "ending discrimination on the basis of sexual orientation...in our immigration laws," saying that current restrictions on homosexual entry "are based on antiquated and erroneous beliefs long since repudiated by leading medical and scientific groups."

While Mondale was criticized by NGTF Executive Director Virginia Apuzzo for "his lack of specific statements on AIDS" and his reluctance to take a clear position in favor of full security clearances for gays, Mondale went out of his way to be accommodating.

Although the Minnesotan noted the "vulnerability...to black-mail" that plagues homosexuals, he did promise to "establish a commission to investigate the merits of current policy in this regard and make recommendations to resolve any civil rights conflict in this policy."

Mondale bragged that his campaign has "openly gay and lesbian... staff," and that "We are including and recruiting openly gay and lesbian candidates on our delegate slates." He added, "I have actively sought and will continue to seek the votes of gay men and lesbians. I have so far received endorsements from the Gertrude Stein Democratic Club of Washington, D.C., and the Lambda Independent Democrats of Brookly [N.Y.], and hope to win support from other such groups."

■ The National Organization for Women, that fervently pro-abortion, pro-ERA outfit which strongly backs Walter Mondale, sponsored a "first-of-its-kind" national Lesbian confab in Milwaukee from January 20-22. Topics addressed included "Lesbian and Gay Candidates and Campaigns," "Coming Out in NOW," "Minority Rights and Lesbian Rights," and "Recruiting Lesbians to NOW."

"In addition to holding the conference to exchange ideas between NOW's national leadership and its largely visible Lesbian membership," the homosexual weekly *The Washington Blade* reported, "the conference served as a symbolic gesture of NOW's 'renewal of our commitment'" to homosexual rights, according to NOW boss Judy Goldsmith. Commented the *Blade:*

"NOW also put some teeth into that commitment by carrying out a resolution, passed at its last national convention, to target one state [New Jersey] to throw NOW resources and clout behind a gay rights bill."

*Human Events*
February 25, 1984

## Appendix 32

Democratic front-runner Walter Mondale has, for the first time, endorsed a federal "gay rights" bill that would open both public and private schools to homosexual teachers, gym instructors and guidance counselors.

As we noted last week in our story on Mondale's courting of the gay vote, the former Vice President endorsed a wide range of pro-homosexual measures in answer to a questionnaire issued by the National Gay Task Force, but stopped short of advocating the federal gay rights bill. He said simply that he supported the legislation "in concept."

But on February 16, just a few days before the Iowa caucuses, Mondale endorsed the measure. The announcement came at a Susan B. Anthony reception sponsored by the pro-abortion, pro-homosexual, National Organization for Women.

*The Washington Blade,* the homosexual newspaper in the Nation's Capital, told this story in a revealing article by Lou Chibbaro Jr., which carried the headline: "Iowa Activists Busy Behind-the-Scenes."

"Gay rights has been a subject on the minds of Iowa campaign organizers of a least four presidential candidates, including the Iowa campaign of former President Mondale...," Chibbaro reported.

"Yet this fact," he continued, "has not been reported in the local or national press even though throngs of reporters have been scouring the Iowa countryside for fresh angles in their coverage of the much-heralded Iowa presidential caucuses."

Among Chibbaro's revelations:

■ At least 200 gay activists—about 100 of them openly homosexual—ran as candidates for delegates to the Democratic party convention in the Iowa caucuses.

■ California Sen. Alan Cranston "has hired two openly gay persons to his Iowa campaign staff, aggressively recruited gay volunteers from all over the state, and distributed a detailed position paper that strongly supports gay rights."

■ Gays were "encouraged to participate" in the Mondale campaign and Eann Rains, head of the Lesbian Task Force of the NOW Iowa chapter, "was hired to travel across the state to strengthen support for Mondale..."

■ The campaign of Colorado Sen. Gary Hart "also encouraged gay volunteers..."

As for the other candidates, Chibbaro said the Washington headquarters of the Hollings campaign "called Gay Iowans in an effort to recruit local organizers and caucus participants" and that "some gays" joined the campaigns of George McGovern and Jesse Jackson.

But Mondale turned out to be the big winner, and his announcement, just a few days before the caucuses, of his support of the federal gay rights bill may have contributed to the very weak finish of Alan Cranston, who had been the other strong favorite of the homosexuals.

NOW trumpeted Mondale's endorsement of the bill in a news release that quoted NOW boss Judy Goldsmith as praising Mondale for "his commitment to economic and social justice to all Americans, including millions of lesbians and gay men who will no longer tolerate second-class citizenship."

Mondale was quoted as saying, "I have consistently indicated my support for a legislative remedy to the problem of discrimination. It is clear that the Moynihan bill, S 430, is a carefully crafted piece of legislation and represents the best solution."

In fact, S 430 is sponsored by Sen. Paul Tsongas (D.-Mass.), with Sen. Patrick Moynihan (D.-N.Y.) as a co-sponsor. The other Senate co-sponsors are Robert Packwood (R.-Ore.), Edward Kennedy (D.-Mass.), Daniel Inouye (D.-Hawaii), Spark Matsunaga (D.-Hawaii) and presidential aspirants Ernest Hollings (D.-S.C.) and Alan Cranston (D.-Calif.).

The bill would amend the 1964 Civil Rights Act to prohibit discrimination in employment based on "sexual orientation." It is not as broad as the gay rights bill in the House, sponsored by Rep. Ted Weiss (D.-N.Y.), which covers employment, public accommodations and housing. That bill has 75 co-sponsors.

The Senate bill, nevertheless, would have far-reaching implications. It would apply to hiring, promotions and fringe benefits in both public and private employment. The bill exempts no institutions, not even religious schools.

Jeff Levi, the Washington representative of the National Gay Task Force, told *Human Events* that the bill would "presumably" also cover federal agencies like the CIA and even the military—occupations normally denied to homosexuals because of their susceptibility to blackmail by the enemy.

Levi said the bill specifically says that affirmative action won't be used to guarantee homosexuals rights in employment, but the 1964 Civil Rights Act, as history demonstrates, has been used to promote the use of both affirmative action and quotas, despite pledges of its sponsors that this could never happen.

Columnist Pat Buchanan has said the issue of gay rights is "social dynamite" and it could do for Walter Mondale what busing did for George McGovern" in 1972.

The question is: How long will the national media cover up the pandering of the Democratic candidates to the militant homosexual movement?

*Human Events*
March 3, 1984

# Order Form

Concerned citizens who value moral standards and who believe the pen is mightier than the sword can greatly influence their communities and the nation.

Multiply your influence by giving *The Homosexual Revolution: A Look at the Preachers and Politicians Behind It* to friends, relatives, neighbors, clergy, teachers and libraries.

| | |
|---|---|
| 1 copy - $4.95 | 100 copies - $250.00 |
| 2 copies - $8.00 | 500 copies - $1,000.00 |
| 10 copies - $35.00 | 1000 copies - $1,500.00 |
| 25 copies - $75.00 | |

Summit Press
P.O. Box 207
Manitou Springs, CO 80829

Gentlemen:

Send me _____ copies of *The Homosexual Revolution: A Look at the Preachers and Politicians Behind It*.

Payment of $_____ is enclosed (send check or money order). Add $.75 postage & handling, plus $.25 for each additional book ordered. Larger orders will be billed shipping costs.

Name _____

Street_____

City _____

State/Zip _____

We also recommend: *The Homosexual Network* by Rev. Enrique T. Rueda, $13.95, and *Gay Is Not Good* by Dr. Frank duMas, $11.95 (available from Summit Ministries).